WHY
SMART
TEENS
HURT

Other books by Eric Maisel

Why Smart People Hurt
Redesign Your Mind
The Great Book of Journaling (edited with Lynda Monk)

WHY
SMART
TEENS
HURT

Helping Adolescents Cope
with the Consequences of Intelligence

ERIC MAISEL

Conari Press

Coral Gables, FL

Cover Design: Elina Diaz
Layout & Design: Carmen Fortunato

For permission requests, please contact the publisher at:
Mango Publishing Group
2850 S Douglas Road, 4th Floor
Coral Gables, FL 33134 USA
info@mango.bz

For special orders, quantity sales, course adoptions and corporate sales, please email the publisher at sales@mango.bz. For trade and wholesale sales, please contact Ingram Publisher Services at customer.service@ingramcontent.com or +1.800.509.4887.

Why Smart Teens Hurt: Helping Adolescents Cope with the Consequences of Intelligence

Library of Congress Cataloging-in-Publication number: 2022937647
ISBN: (print) 978-1-64250-997-7, (ebook) 978-1-64250-998-4
BISAC: FAM043000, FAMILY & RELATIONSHIPS / Life Stages / Teenagers

Table of Contents

INTRODUCTION

My focus in this book is on the special challenges that smart teens face. I am interested in helping smart teens and their parents because smart teens are the ones who as adults will have the job of keeping civilization afloat. They will desalinate sea water, create vaccines, write novels that move hearts and engage minds, and stand up to fascists. They are our most important resource—and they are hurting.

One of my goals is to name and describe the challenges that smart teens face. A second goal is to not objectify teens but rather to try to communicate what it feels like to be *inside* their reality. For this reason, I intend to talk directly to teens in each lesson, as well as to their parents. A teen isn't "someone with ADHD" or "someone with bipolar disorder." A smart teen is a rich, alive, thoughtful, often troubled person. I want the teens who read this book to feel heard and seen.

Maybe you are one of those smart teens. What does it feel like when you find your overactive brain racing and you have trouble doing things in a calm, settled way? How often does that racing lead to disorganization, procrastination, a sense of inner chaos, and real-world failures like poor grades? What does it feel like to have your imagination shut down because you need to learn facts for the test?

How will you react when your natural curiosity is met with hostility and you're instructed to stop asking impertinent questions? Or what will your response be when you receive mixed and deeply unsettling messages about how smart you are, on the one hand, and about how incompetent and unworthy you are, on the other? What does all this *feel* like? And what are the likely results?

I hope that this book will prove something of a voyage of discovery, helping you to understand what it's like to inhabit the racing and tempestuous mind of a smart teen. It is wild and unsettled in there. Even if your smart teen is just sitting there morosely, inside, their consciousness is teeming with mental activity. Their sleep is not untroubled, and their thoughts are likely not self-friendly. Their dirty laundry strewn everywhere in their room is a metaphor: their life may well be feeling like that.

Smart teens face the same challenges that all teens are bound to face, like peer pressure, and other challenges that only some teens have to face, like a history of abuse. There may be problems with alcohol and drugs; dealing with bullying and cyber bullying; alienation and hopelessness; stress and anxiety; social media and gaming excesses; self-doubt and self-criticism; and power struggles and battles with parents. There are also the pressures of poverty, the realities of parental discord and divorce, gloomy forecasts about the future of the world, and more.

On top of these, smart teens have their own special challenges. Those are the subject of this book. These include a special, complicated relationship to excellence, an often-abiding sense of being in the completely wrong place, an inability to find anything worth focusing on, existential sadness arising from a clear, unvarnished understanding of the facts of existence, and a poignant hunger for a life aligned with the phrase "truth, beauty, and goodness," a life that does not seem at all available to them.

Of course, to chat about these matters puts us squarely in the minefields of the intelligence debates. But let us picture ourselves as able to levitate over those debates and not get caught up in quagmires like, "What is intelligence?" and "How dare you call someone smarter than someone else!" and "But aren't there many 'intelligences'?" We don't need to define "talented," "gifted," "intelligent," or any of the other words in the family of smart. Let us keep it this simple: If this book speaks to you, it speaks to you. That will be enough.

But I do need to say a few words about the following. When I say "smart," do I also mean "creative"? Those two ideas are often conflated. Interesting studies from long ago attempted to answer the question, "Are there differences between smart students and creative students?" The answer appeared to be an unequivocal "yes." The teachers surveyed had very clear ideas about how the first group differed from the second.

In their view, non-creative smart students had very conventional attitudes and outlooks, leaned right rather than left, tended to pick money-making professions, and rather than delving deeply into subjects, demanded to be told what they needed to know for the test. They were smart but incurious and literal rather than imaginative. If they raised their hand, it was only to ask a question like, "Do we need to remember that?"

The smart teen who will become a sharp corporate lawyer is not the same person as the smart teen who will become an esoteric essayist. "Smart teens" are not a monolithic group, and an ability to think is not the same as a desire to create. It follows that not all of the challenges we'll discuss will fall equally on the shoulders of every smart teen. Let us keep that in mind as we look at the fifty challenges we're about to explore.

The world is wobbling. We can't expect a smart, angst-ridden teen to step up and put that wobbly world on her shoulders. They can perhaps barely manage to get out of bed! And still, we want to do everything in our power to help that teen survive her teenage years and become the person we so desperately need her to be: not a comic book superhero but an apostle of civilization, a committed individual who cares and who tries. May this book help smart teens navigate the maddeningly difficult years of adolescence.

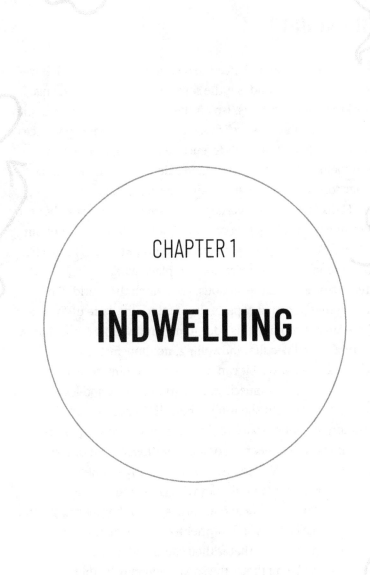

CHAPTER 1

INDWELLING

Indwelling

A mind must be experienced to be understood. We each have that experience—and is it the same for each of us? It seems hard to believe that it is. Isn't it the case that differences in the thing called "intelligence" must produce different experiences of mind? Mustn't those differences amount to differences in remembering, in imagining, in calculating, and in all the other sorts of things that a brain causes a mind to do?

Hard science does perhaps have something to say about differences in calculating or remembering, but that is not our subject. We are focusing on what it feels like and is like to be in the room that is your mind, that place where you get sad, create stories, become anxious, and watch the world. I'm calling that personal experience of mind, the state of "being there" in the room that is your mind, "indwelling." It is that particular and peculiar indwelling, not how fast a brain can calculate or how well it can memorize, that interests us.

A smart teen is muscle and heart and arms and legs and all the rest, but she is most herself "in her mind." That creation, the inner space of the mind, is where she pesters herself about the meaning of life, talks herself out of learning to drive, writes a whole novel in an evening but never gets a word down on paper, argues with God, and sees herself in Rome, looking for love and a warm spot for her morning latte.

Whereas her less "mind-oriented" peers may spend less time in the room that is their mind and may even feel resistance to being there, the smart teen may be there constantly; it is where she lives. It has a look to it (maybe a dark and claustrophobic look), a feel to it (maybe a sad and heavy feel), a rhythm to it (maybe a pressurized and racing rhythm), and all sorts of returning contents with names like thoughts, worries, memories, and fantasies.

If we don't acknowledge, honor, and try to understand the centrality of this experience of mind, we will have no idea what is going on "in" or "with" a smart teen. It would be like trying to understand what a computer "really is" without the concept of programming, or attempting to comprehend how a skyscraper stands up without the concept of a foundation. Indwelling is foundational, fundamental, and our primary subject.

A smart teen suffers for all of the usual reasons and in all of the usual ways that any teen suffers. But his particular pain is that he lives in a room, his mind, that is flooded with thoughts and feelings that pester him, pressure him, and leave him little respite. A powerful steam engine that is functioning keeps producing steam, even if you don't want that steam. A smart teen's powerful brain keeps producing all sorts of thinking—from funny riddles to self-recriminations, from fragments of poetry to imagined slights—at a relentless pace. Indwelling is not a joy; it is rather a tense condition.

A smart teen is obliged to live in that messy, roiling, pressurized place. He has no choice and can't help it, any more than that locomotive can help hurtling along. Is it any wonder that to the world, he might look qualified for a diagnosis of "ADHD," "bipolar," "OCD," or some other simple-to-affix label? But he is not a "symptom picture." If he is like many smart teens, he is on a wild ride, one invisible to observers, and that is the crux of the matter.

For Parents

When your smart teen is locked away in her room, she is really locked away in her own mind. She is living in her mind, a place where solar storms are raging, where fantastic animals are created and annihilated, where loud conversations are held, where numbers are juggled for no earthly reason. Yes, she is also simultaneously watching television, texting, listening to music, surfing the Net, and doing her homework. But all of that is on the surface and superficial. What is going on behind and around all that is what makes up both her experience of her own mind and her experience of life.

She looks to be doing her homework while listening to music; but more fundamentally, she is indwelling in the wild world that is her mind. Why emphasize this? Because we have lost touch with this core reality. Parents are pushed to focus on their child's abilities on the one hand and on his or her behaviors on the other. But what about her mind? What about her experience of indwelling? What about what is actually going on in there? That is so worth our attention!

For Teens

The world has its dominant ways of talking about what's "wrong" with a person. A person who looks a certain way or feels a certain way is defined as having a "mental disorder" or "mental disease." He or she "has an Internet addiction" or "lacks social skills" or "keeps himself isolated." He or she is "difficult" or "traveling with the wrong crowd" or "on the spectrum." Not a single one of these ways of speaking acknowledges or even hints at the reality of indwelling: the reality that a person has a mind. It is *there* that the dramas unfold.

In this book, we are going to take your mind seriously. To put it another way, we are going to be "psychological." We are going to try to get at what it feels like to have a racing mind, as so many smart teens do; what it feels like to simultaneously feel very special and very small, what it feels like to face hard work and to shy away from it, and all those other indwelling events that make up the reality of your life. The world may want to look *at* you (and do things to you): We are going to visit inside where you indwell, where you really reside.

Solitude

How can a straightforward line like "I want to be alone" become iconic and famous the world over? What mysterious something did Greta Garbo capture when she uttered that oh-so-ordinary line in the 1932 film *Grand Hotel*? I'm pretty sure that it became such a known phrase because it spoke to the startling desire for solitude lurking in the heart of just about every person of a certain sort, the kind of person who will go on to be a novelist, a monk, a research scientist, a sculptor, a game designer, a yogi, or a professor of history. That line spoke volumes.

Such a desire for solitude is made up of several parts. First, there is the obsessive need to indwell: to be in the room that is one's mind. There is a *need* to dive into that thousand-page history of the Byzantine Empire, to dream up a story, to listen to music because music is brewing inside, to be reading, thinking, and listening, to be living in one's own heaven and hell. This is a need perhaps greater than any other need. We may well want to recalibrate any "hierarchy of needs" list and assign indwelling to its rightful place.

Second, there is a wise wariness about being with people. If you do not see value in sitting among dull people and chatting about the abundance of rain or the lack of rain or anything about rain, if you experience that as not just a waste of time but as existentially painful, as if you were actually killing your time on earth, then you have no reason on earth to be there. For many people, the majority of smart teens included, it can feel much more existentially rich and much more appropriate to be in one's mind than to be in idle company.

Third, there is world-building going on in solitude, a learning energy, a creative energy, a building energy, as, for instance, a teen draws her peculiar cast of characters, posts them on social media, gets followers and likes and an audience, and creates a complete, vibrant world.

This world-building can only be done in solitude. That is the only place where that can get done, which makes solitude as valuable to a smart person as water and air.

A teen's permanently closed door with its "Keep Out!" sign is a cliché. Like many clichés, it reflects a distinct truth: Teens want to listen to their music, wander the Net, fantasize, talk to their friends, crawl under the covers, and, well, just be left alone. They want their solitude so that they can indwell. They need it; yet at the same time, it can be a seriously dangerous place. It is home to first novels, but it is also a breeding ground for fevers. A parent may well sense this even if her smart teen does not.

For Parents

Your smart teen needs her alone time. At the same time, it is easy for that isolation, social distancing, and fierce demand for solitude to go too far. Indwelling is valuable, wonderful, and necessary. It can also be a place of nightmares, unhealthy obsessions, and darkness. Therefore, you will want to coax your smart teen out into the light. She may not want to come; she may moan and groan, or she may flat-out refuse. But she still needs the light, fresh air, and relationships. Be a little clever and a little adamant and see if you can tease your smart teen out into the world of people.

If, when you get her out, she is silent and distant, if she wants to sit on the sidelines and observe, in short, if she wants to bring her solitude with her as if she hasn't really left her mindroom at all, be as engaging as you know how to be—which may be as much a stretch for you as it is for her. You may be exactly like her, craving your own solitude. This outing, which may be tense, silent, or awkward, may be as much a stretch for you as for her. Make it happen anyway. Give both of you the chance to stretch in the direction of relationship.

For Teens

In solitude, symphonies are created. In solitude, minds run amok. You will have the lifelong job of making sure that you both get to "be in your head" when you need and want to be and that you also "get out of your head" so frequently and so well that wonderful solitude doesn't become cold, alienating, painful isolation.

There is no formula for maintaining the right amounts of solitude and relationship. What you can do, however, is put up a bright neon exit sign in your mindroom, one that reminds you that you can get out and that you ought to get out. You can add some cheerful internal musical alert, one that signals that it is time to think about whether it is time to leave your mindroom. And you can in other ways honor the truth that you had better not make your solitude pervasive and uninterruptible.

Strict solitude—demanding to be alone at all costs—can lead to all sorts of negatives, among them grandiosity, painful overthinking, an inability to empathize, and deep staleness. Of course, you want your solitude: It is where you think, create, and dream. But be careful; if you do not come up for air and out for life, you will have transformed your mindroom into something resembling a prison cell. You do not want that to happen.

I've put this section after indwelling because they of course connect. The main challenge of indwelling is that your experience there be a positive one and not a negative one, that you don't end up with a mind that feels like a bed of nails. The main challenge of solitude is that as much as you may crave it, it's important that you don't turn it into a sort of holy grail. Solitude is wonderful—and dangerous. There is more to life than "I want to be alone." You may have to talk yourself into believing that: and if you do have to do some self-convincing, make sure that you do exactly that.

Racing

We say that "thoughts race" and that "the mind races." These phrases capture something of the experience of indwelling, but not enough of it. It is rather as if one's whole being is racing, which can make it hard to sit still, concentrate, focus on a question, or feel settled. When that racing is in the service of some productive obsession like getting your novel written, that is one thing. But even then, that racing is often more like pressure than bliss. Picture an inexperienced rider clinging to a racehorse at full gallop. That is neither easy nor pleasant.

It is your very being that is sending your mind off racing. This racing comes about as a result of your human energy, your need to live, and the necessity of using your brain to make sense of life. Those human requirements send your mind spinning; and then, having been handed the task and told to gallop, your racing mind takes over, holding your very being hostage.

This common dynamic, one faced by many smart teens, is like getting on a train because you must and then discovering, as the train starts hurtling faster and faster, that there is no engineer and no brakeman. At an extreme, when this pressurized racing infuses your whole being, we call it "mania," as if that label explains much of anything. No, "mania" is just a word; what we need is an explanation of this evolutionary process that produces reckless energy that must then be dissipated. Even more than that, we need tactics to deal with this primordial challenge.

To complicate matters further, there appears to be a natural connection between this racing, with its pressurized feel and its demands, and a sad sort of opposite where we lose energy and motivation and want to do anything but race. It is as if one minute we were running a race with all our might; and then suddenly, in the next minute, we stopped caring about crossing the finish line and just plopped down by the side of the road. Something happens internally—something in the realm of the "psychological"—and the race suddenly seems irrelevant.

You can of course see the outline of the thing called "bipolar disorder" in this human dynamic. But that label, like the label "mania," just turns a spectacularly human process into something along the lines of broken plumbing. We are not talking here about a mental disorder, a neurotransmitter problem, or faulty wiring. Rather, we are talking about a certain challenge that occurs because of the way the brain breaks the bounds of its instructions. It is charged with handling life; it finds that charge daunting; and like a wild horse corralled, it kicks at the fence, until finally, crashing through, it flies off like the wind.

For Parents

Even if your smart teen is doing nothing at all, even if he or she is just slouched on the sofa lost in space, it is rather likely that this "racing" dynamic is lurking just out of sight somewhere. This dynamism is ready to propel your teen into something obsessive as the train that she has boarded suddenly starts hurtling along.

What can this hurtling look like? It can manifest as chronic insomnia; your teen talking in such a way that you can't get in a word edgewise; plans made and suddenly abandoned; passionate enthusiasms followed quickly by a loss of interest; or even irritability that looks like a toothache or an earache but is actually a *brain*-ache. As different as these faces of the problem may look, they are related, connected by the way that racing brain dynamics play themselves out in human beings.

What can you do? At a minimum, you can make an offering based on your best understanding of what might constitute long-term help for a racing brain. If, for example, you have the sense that meditation might help, invite your teen to take a meditation class with you. Will he groan, make a face, or in some other way decline? Quite likely; but it is still good to have made the offer. Making that offer shows your teen three things: that you are thinking about him; that you are willing to put yourself out; and that you appreciate that a racing mind is a terrific challenge.

For Teens

The picture I'm painting here may not pertain to every smart teen, but it may well be relevant to you. A racing brain, a racing mind, and a racing being mean that you are alive and percolating, that your life energy is bubbling, and that your gears are whirring; that is the upside. The downside is that all this can also amount to grave danger. That racing energy can prevent human interactions. It can produce tremendous noise, drowning out your own good thoughts. It can produce an inner mind ache, turning your thoughts dark and brooding and making it impossible to really think. Just as natural appetite can end up as gluttony, natural brain activity can end up as the physiological equivalent of electrical overload and fuses blowing.

Insofar as it is humanly possible, you want to get a grip on all this, because a hurtling train without an engineer or brakeman can't stop at any station, there is no way off, and it may leave the rails at the next sharp curve. There are only imperfect tactics for achieving that grip: hot showers, journaling, meditation, breathing exercises, "redesign your mind" techniques, and maybe psychiatric chemicals (but they are a very double-edged sword). However, the first line of defense is becoming aware that this mental racing really is a challenge.

It is not a great help to simply put a label like "bipolar disorder," "mania," "obsessive-compulsive disorder," "ADD," or "ADHD" on this racing dynamic. Such labeling accomplishes nothing. What you want for yourself, if you can pull it off, is an understanding of your own racing nature. Why are you racing, rushing, and hurtling? Is it a defensive flight from painful knowledge? Is it a fired-up imagination bouncing off the walls from one fragmentary idea to the next? Is it some mélange of passions, worries, excitement, and self-condemnation, all coming together as chaos? Can you tease this apart?

You are smart. Here is a place to apply your intelligence. There is no subject more fascinating, more difficult, more elusive, or more important than the way that high intelligence converts into problematic racing energy for many smart teens. You do not want to make an unfortunate journey from living with a brain that could do good work, one that could race along at just the right clip, to a tumultuous brain heading for a crack-up.

No one has perfect answers here. But at least you are well positioned to witness your own dynamics, think (even as you race) about what may be going on, and create some kind of metaphorical dashboard that allows you to gain some control over all that racing. Pick an image—a jockey on a powerful racehorse, a brakeman on a hurtling locomotive—and try to get a real felt sense of exactly what this challenge is. It has to do with life energy and how that energy is transmuted, not into gold, but into pressure. You are obliged to deal with that pressure, or else it will rule you.

CHAPTER 2

DECEPTION

The Emperor's New Clothes

Tyrants always target smart people first because smart people can see through their deceptions. From childhood, a smart child will start shaking her head as she sees and hears things that make no sense to her. She may voice her sentiments and point a finger, or she may keep quiet out of fear or shyness, but either way she will have a disquieting inner experience. She shakes her head and wonders, "Why on earth are people saying this?" and "Why on earth are people doing this?" She can't really stop herself from shaking her head, because she is genuinely perplexed, astounded...and offended.

Margaret, a coaching client, explains: "Yes, I was *that* child. One of my earliest memories of seeing through falsehood is from primary school. Living in a British Commonwealth country, back then, we learned about the monarchy. I clearly recall my internal response to learning that kings and queens used to believe they ruled by divine decree. What rubbish, I thought. Why would a six-year-old have known to think that? But I did. I was the kid always asking why, challenging the accepted narrative, and trying to do things my way. I guess I just hated that sort of lying; and maybe more than the lie, the general acceptance of the lie. How could *so many people* buy such nonsense? I've been troubled by that question my whole life."

It is one thing to see through some minor deception. Maybe that can be ignored or tolerated. But when the deceit is massive, responding to it can easily become a lifelong obsession. Let a smart teen see through a false master narrative like, "Poor folks get a fair shake in the criminal justice system," or "God has His reasons for gathering folks to die in plane crashes," or "Being bored is a medical disorder treatable with drugs," and she may organize her whole life around disputing and debunking that narrative and/or serving those harmed by that narrative.

Where does that sharp public defender come from, the one who could make a fortune in the corporate world but who accepts peanuts to defend the poor? She is doing her poorly paying job because she knows that it is simply false that all people are treated equally in the criminal justice system. She knows that mandatory minimum sentences are racist and hypocritical, she knows that the criminal justice system is not color-blind, and she feels a moral obligation to act on her sure knowledge. Could she have made an easier life for herself? Yes, certainly. But she sees what she sees and finds it impossible to turn a blind eye to the truth.

A smart teen's whole life can become organized around responding *with her life* to society's untruths. The fact that she can and will see through falsity is no idle matter. In fact, in practical terms, when it comes to how she will make a living and how she will lead her life, nothing may matter more. Her smarts supply her with a penetrating gaze, she sees what she sees, she finds that spectacle intolerable, and she must either bravely respond or disappoint herself by not responding.

For Parents

How this issue plays itself out in your family will have a lot to do with your own relationship to truthfulness and your own relationship to those who prefer deception. If, for example, your husband is an orthodox religious person, while your daughter can't understand how there can be a God who cares what plates you eat on, the seeds are sown for dramatic rifts, massive alienation, and even lifelong estrangement. Can a parent and his or her child end up never speaking to one another over such differences? Yes, of course. It happens all the time. Do you want to say to your smart teen, "Your beliefs offend us and are intolerable to us, so back off or get out!"? Or do you want to love your child? It is not easy to love someone whose beliefs you hate. Is that even possible? If you actually hate a person's beliefs, can you still love that person? What do you think?

Remember: The polluter and the whistleblower are enemies. They don't just have "different opinions." Each wants the other to stop. Each is invested in the other stopping. And each may go to great lengths to force the other to stop. The second I say, "Gosh, are you trying to tell me that lead in our drinking water is somehow okay?" you and I are at more than intellectual odds. Seeing through falsehood is serious business. In real life, it makes the emperor and the small boy in the crowd enemies.

Your smart teen will regularly see through life's platitudes and deceptions, and that will *matter to her*. How do you want to respond?

For Teens

It is an outcome of smartness to see through falsehood, and it is an obligation of conscience to respond to the injustices you see. That is easy to say, but the consequences of these two truths, that you will see through life's charades and that you will feel internally pressured to speak your truth and redress wrongs, can lead to dramatic consequences.

These consequences can include ending up in an honorable profession that pays poorly and provides few psychological or tangible rewards. They can lead to painful challenges like alienation from your own family, ethnic group, religious group, or society. These consequences and challenges are not at all rare in the lives of smart teens.

What does this imply? Does it mean you will want to cultivate a way of stepping aside from this pressure? Could it mean you will need to cultivate a stance that sounds like, "Yes, that is wrong, I can see that. But how do I want to respond? And do I have to respond at all?" Seeing through the pretenses is one thing; that is unavoidable. How you react to seeing through those falsehoods is a different matter entirely.

You can respond, "There is *so much* deception out there, too much for any one person to deal with. Therefore, let me just ignore it and create a meaningful life for myself." Or you can respond, "This bit of lying is really too much, really too dreadful, with too many terrible real-world consequences. So I am going to devote my whole life to resisting it." And you can take different positions in varying circumstances, ignoring some deceptions, reacting in a mild and constrained way to other forms of humbug, and only sometimes throwing yourself "all in."

You may find yourself moving along different points of this continuum as if it were an electric third rail, with each stop its own electrified experience. In the fairy tale, it is an almost comical moment when the little boy cries, while pointing at the naked Emperor, "But he hasn't got anything on!" In the story, the little boy is credited with opening up the whole town's eyes. In real life, wars are fought over less. Take it as a given that you will see through many falsehoods—and that possessing that truth-telling apparatus can get you into all kinds of difficulties.

Science

Whether or not she can name it or describe it, one thing that a smart teen understands intuitively is the scientific method. She understands the idea of trial-and-error experimentation and the difference between a hypothesis and a fact; she comprehends that for a theory to be valid, it must be repeatable and verifiable; and she realizes that paradigms can shift as understanding increases. She may not know any of this formally, but she knows it in her bones.

What is her challenge, then? Her challenge is that the majority of human beings despise science—first, because much of it is beyond them, and second, because they do not want their beliefs undermined. The most obvious sorts of question, the ones that any science-minded investigators would ask right off the bat, like, "Why is your religion more valid than that religion over there?" or, "By what criteria are you judging the validity of the war we are currently fighting?" or, "What solid experiments have been run to prove or disprove the reality of psychic powers?" are hateful to them. They do not want their opinions challenged, and that's what science does.

As a result, every time a smart teen hears some unexamined, unsubstantiated, downright silly thing, some blatant misuse of statistics, some self-serving, self-congratulatory declaration like, "God helped our team to victory," or some absurd claim that hating your government's policies ought to be construed as a mental disorder, she will want to rise up and say, "Gosh, that's pretty ridiculous." And if she does rise up, she will likely be met with hostility.

What, then, to do? Give up on people? Give up on science? Give up?

Even more insidiously, she may well find herself choosing a career where bad science is the norm. Much of the research in the social sciences, while it looks like science, isn't really. Some fields that look exciting—like, say, cognitive science— find amazing ways to not really do science. A smart teen can easily find herself traveling down a road where her intuitive allegiance to the scientific method runs afoul of the pointedly shoddy thinking in her academic specialization. There she may find herself, knowing in her heart that the claims being made around her do not hold water; but as someone playing the game herself, what is she supposed to do?

If she were duller, she might not notice. But she can't help but notice. Even if she wants to dumb herself down so as to get along and play along, part of her will rebel. She will rebel by procrastinating so long on her grant proposal that she will miss the deadline and watch her lab close for lack of funding. For a smart teen, this tension may play itself out everywhere—at the family dinner table, where some non-statistic is made to sound like gospel, with her friends, who are making their decisions based on the Tarot, or in chemistry class, where everything is dumbed down to the level of rotten eggs. She is bound to notice—and what to do?

For Parents

When your teen was a small child, she may have asked many "Why?" questions. That was a young scientist at work. You may have had your own way of explaining how one Santa Claus could get presents to all children everywhere during a single night, or you might have gone with a nonanswer like, "It's all quite magical!" and your little one may have nodded. But was she satisfied with your answer? And was some cognitive dissonance already brewing, some tension between her understanding of rational argument and her confusion about why the world wanted to feed her falsehoods?

There is a question you need to consider: Do you or don't you want to support rationality? Do you want to play "Of course, Santa Claus is real!" games, or are you willing to have conversations that begin with, "Well, let's take a careful look at that"? In small matters and in large matters, do you want your approach to be, "Let's really think about that"? Or are you comfortable setting the bar much lower, where it is usually set, at the level of quick, self-serving, unsubstantiated opinion? Do you want to model rational inquiry—or not?

For Teens

Because of the way your mind works, you will probably find the methods of the thing called "science" convincing. You will find arguments for the roundness of the earth convincing, and you will have no idea what to do with those folks who loudly assert that the earth is flat.

You will likely want to shake some sense into such people, on the one hand, and ignore and dismiss them, on the other hand. But what if that flat-earth advocate is your teacher, your pastor, or your father? Shaking won't work. Will ignoring? What sort of relationship can you have with your father if his basic way of operating is anti-scientific? How about if he feels he can say whatever he likes without justification? What if he not only asserts that the earth is flat but lives his life that way? What sort of relationship can you have with him?

The scientific method is an evidence-gathering and truth-finding apparatus. It is something to love, respect, and preserve. You know that in your heart, but life may throw you curveballs. A time may come when you want to go down some fascinating road where in order to travel to its conclusion, you will be required to suspend your rationality. How will that feel? A time may come when you discover that the field you're in, one that calls itself scientific, really isn't. How will that feel? Yes, $2 + 2 = 4$. But the world is made up of countless irrational numbers. You may find your very allegiance to what science represents challenged. What will you do then?

The Map Is Not the Territory

If you looked at a bell curve or a normal distribution curve mapping intelligence, you would see at a glance that 70 percent of the teenaged population falls in the middle, that 15 percent falls to the left of the middle, and that 15 percent is distributed to the right, where greater intelligence resides. That is easy to see and easy to grasp.

But you wouldn't have learned a thing about that 15 percent as a group—their fears, their worries, their talents, their abilities, or their ways of seeing the world or of organizing information. Likewise, you wouldn't have learned anything about any individual teen in that group. Nor would you have learned what "smart" is, what that word is supposed to connote or signify.

That curve—that map—would be visually arresting but would tell you nothing about what was being measured, if what was being measured (namely, "intelligence") was a valid construct, or what it was like to be a member of that group. Would that map tell you much, if anything, about the territory? Not really. But it would still sit there as if something large had been communicated.

You might look to other maps—say, brain scans—and possibly find yourself mesmerized by the imagery there. Oh, there's a smart teen's brain. How interesting! But would you have learned anything particularly useful? You would not. If you were looking for lesions, that would be one thing. That would likely be the right map for that territory. But smarts? A brain scan can't map that territory.

Early in the twentieth century the mathematician Eric Temple Bell remarked, "The map is not the thing mapped." The philosopher and engineer Alfred Korzybski, acknowledging his debt to Bell, created the catchier phrase, "The map is not the territory," to represent the idea that a model of reality is not reality itself. In an equally memorable way, Alan Watts produced the epigram, "The menu is not the meal." All agreed that maps have their utility, but if and only if they correctly depict the territory.

Would a map depicting a flat earth, fantastical sea creatures, and made-up land masses much help a mariner? Definitely not! Bad maps do more harm than good.

This truth matters. A smart teen is likely to come to see that many of the maps foisted upon her are invalid, and will likely also conclude that even the valid ones often do not provide good information about the territory being mapped. She will come to see that mapmaking is a convenient resource for those who would deceive and that every map must be scrutinized to make sure that it isn't just humbug. Does this mean that she must lead with skepticism? Yes, it does.

Society's mapmakers are very powerful and influential. The mapmakers who get to legislate the naming of what might be bothering smart teens (and everyone else) have created an atlas called the Diagnostic and Statistical Manual of the American Psychiatric Association. That atlas portrays a world of imaginary mental disorder islands, each one separated from the next, inviting you to believe, for instance, that your sadness at the glaciers melting away and your angry opposition to environmental exploitation have no connection. Really?

Both parents and teens are pressured nowadays into believing that the mental health map that a professional class has created—a map with islands called "clinical depression" and "attention deficit hyperactivity disorder" and "adjustment disorder" and "oppositional defiant disorder"—is a valid depiction of a territory. It isn't, but that is the paradigm—the map—that has won the race, and every smart teen and his or her parent is affected by it.

These are quite abstract ideas, the deceitful misapprehensions of invalid maps and the insufficiency of all maps. But while abstract, they are nevertheless vitally important ideas. For instance, a college catalogue is a map; and if it incorrectly portrays the territory a student is about to traverse, that may amount to four wasted years and even the wrong profession. If you can manage not to confuse that catalogue with the college experience that it is trying to portray, whether it is an honorable and accurate or dishonorable and inaccurate portrayal, your clarity of perspective can give you a fighting chance to make the best decisions possible.

For Parents

Your smart teen is likely to approach life from the vantage point of skepticism, and that is appropriate. There is much to be skeptical about, given the relentless marketing and promoting of this or that agenda. You, too, may want to lead with skepticism, say when the learning specialist at your smart teen's school wants to label him based on some makeshift test, some teacher reports, and an allegiance to the mental disorder paradigm.

It can feel daunting if your smart teen has her doubts about just about everything. But that relentless doubting arises because she is built to dispute untruthfulness. She may overdo it; but it is good that she is observant and analytical. Better that she deconstructs too much than move through life naively, buying one master narrative after another.

For Teens

You will be presented with many maps in life, and many
of them may strike you as suspicious. Trust your instincts.
If you're presented with a map of history, you are right to
suspect that the map was written by history's victors. If you're
presented with a particular map of mental illness, you are
right to suspect that pharmaceutical companies are lurking
in the background. Many if not most of the maps that you'll
be presented with are likely invalid. Those invalid maps
constitute a monumental deception that may forever rankle
whenever you are confronted with them.

And even the better maps, the ones that are valid and
reasonable, are still only maps and not the territory. The
menu is never the meal. This means that you must be vigilant
and skeptical, which also means that you may find yourself
more on your guard in life than you would like to be. Must
every map really be poked and deconstructed? Well, a pretty
brochure is not a vacation. A course description is not a class.
A brain scan is not a mind. Mapmakers have their agendas;
and you have your sharp eyes with which to spot them.

CHAPTER 3

IMPERFECTION

Nothing Less Than Perfect

Many smart teens do sloppy work because nothing less than perfect will do. This sounds upside-down, doesn't it? But it makes perfect psychological sense. If you know that perfection is unattainable, why expend all that energy doing something merely decent, which neither you nor the world will find acceptable, when you can just take it easy and skate along? Why spend hour after hour practicing the violin when you know that you are not going to sound like Isaac Stern at the end of all that practicing?

Why not just shrug instead, and maybe play a video game or read a good book? Internally, this sounds like, "If I can't do it perfectly, why bother? Let me take it easy." But a smart teen operating this way is rather more likely to end up feeling queasy rather than easy. His rationale for doing a poor job ends up feeling like a rationalization. Deep down inside, he would really prefer to do good work rather than the shoddy work he is doing. Harpooned by the word "perfect," he now finds himself in one version of the anxiety state known as "perfectionism."

In that state, he makes a hash of things, lowers his self-esteem, and heightens his anxiety. At the same time, he misses learning an important lesson about tolerating the process and begins to drop things at the first hint of difficulty. He picks up tennis, finds it hard, and drops it. He begins writing his first novel, hates his first paragraphs, and drops it. He finds it impossible to learn calculus without really studying, and since he's become unpracticed at studying and is currently incapable of giving studying his all, he begins failing his calculus exams.

People who are accomplished at anything have learned that "perfect" is the enemy of the good. The smart teen I'm describing has made an enemy of "good" as well as "perfect" and has landed in the sad place of the shoddy. Little kids in team sports get participation trophies just for playing. Our smart teen has moved beyond participation trophies and into the world that can be summarized, "Since one error is a catastrophe, let me make countless errors and be done with the good." So as to guard against the experience of failure, he stops participating.

Then there are the smart teens who are actually and actively striving for perfection, who hunger to rid their work of every error and blemish, and who will stay up until dawn getting their term paper just right, with no comma out of place and every margin perfect. This teen puts herself under the sort of enormous pressure that only the specter of the flawless can produce.

The first teen is suffering from one version of perfectionism, the "I've thrown in the towel" version. The second teen is suffering from a different version of perfectionism, the "I will work myself to the bone" version. Both are anxious in their own way, caught up in dramas created by the word "perfect." The first, holding back, may never learn that the good can lead to the great. The second, striving forward, may achieve work of the highest order, but at what cost?

For Parents

As an adult, you have learned that "perfect" is not the bullseye. Not only is virtually nothing ever perfect, not only are the majority of things average to mediocre, but even when something is so-to-speak perfect—a perfectly cooked piece of salmon, or that perfect phrase for the wedding toast—it is lovely but ultimately of passing value. Values like love and freedom and engagement and happiness are many rungs higher up the ladder.

Of course, you do not want to sell your teen on the idea that shoddy work is okay. But do you want to sell him on "perfect" as the way? Do you want your mantra to be "Perfect or the highway"? Or do you want to paint a different picture of life, one where happiness counts, where showing up is its own kind of brilliance, and where excellence rather than perfection is the high bar for which to strive? Doesn't that sound better than a life of not trying, on the one hand, or frightful stress on the other?

For Teens

In *Hope in the Dark*, Rebecca Solnit coins a lovely phrase: "Perfection is a stick with which to beat the possible." Do you have that image in mind, of the possible being abused by the stick of perfection? Let us chase that stick out of the room, chase it out of the house, and chase it right into the blazing fire burning in our backyard fire pit. Let perfection burn in heck! We can still revere excellence (see the next section), but we need never be beaten about the head and shoulders by perfection again.

If you would like to carve out a suitable place for yourself along the continuum from poor to perfect, where stops along the way have names like mediocre, average, good, and excellent, set your sights on the good, and rest assured that the good will lead to the excellent. Your affirmation could be: "Let me do good work, let me allow for mistakes and messes, let me revere excellence without stressing out about it, and let me banish perfection from my vocabulary." Transform that insidious "nothing less than perfect" into a rousing "something less than perfect!" Remember: That stick of perfection is just smoldering ashes now.

Excellence

"Excellence" sounds like a word out of the world of marketing, promoting, advertising, and humbug. It gets tossed around with words like "new" and "improved" and "great" and comes with lots of exclamation points. In our global embrace of late-stage capitalism, who isn't hawking something "excellent," whether it's an air fryer, an electric car, a mutual fund, or a way to turn lead into gold?

And yet for smart people, and maybe for smart teens especially, "excellence" means something very real, pressing, and special. It is the high bar to which they consciously or unconsciously aspire. They read a really good novel and whisper, "That was excellent," and they want something like that for themselves.

It might be excellence in science, as they try to picture someone actually inventing calculus or arriving at the relationship between energy, mass, and the speed of light. Now, that's excellent! It might be excellence in the movies, as they come out of the trance of watching a film that is so exceptional it is hard to believe it could have been made by a mere mortal. It might be excellence in dance, as they watch the visiting Bolshoi Ballet.

First comes that experience of inspiration; next comes all the tangled difficulty. This can include chasing excellence but never producing great work; never being given the opportunity to excel; or seeing excellence in the work of others but not crediting excellence in your own. The challenges can also manifest as doing excellent work sometimes, but so rarely that you are always pining for it and constantly half-disappointed in your own efforts; rejecting excellence as a chimera, a fraud, a kind of humbug—yet still pining for it; or envying those who pull it off, and especially envying those who do excellent work in your chosen field. Or it could be doing excellent work but not being recognized for it, perhaps while seeing others do mediocre work that is hailed as excellent. And there are more.

I've worked with many clients who regularly do excellent work but who never feel that they have done enough. For them, excellence hasn't felt excellent enough. Nor has it produced the kind of residual satisfaction that would allow a person to say, "I am still aglow from having done that." That glow is gone almost in an instant, like a candle snuffed out by a cold gust of wind. What is left is a kind of emptiness as the chase begins again. And really, once you have come up with a theory of relativity, how are you supposed to top that? What are the next forty years of your academic career supposed to look like or be about?

Can smart teens be expected to see any of this clearly, given that most smart adults can't? And those smart adults have actual experiences to go on! No, we can't expect a smart teen to know, or even suspect, the amazingly large part that her relationship to excellence is going to play in her life. She opens her browser, lands somewhere, sees a gorgeously lit and composed image, instantly comprehends its excellence— will that moment determine how she will spend her life? It might. When the music of the spheres starts playing, isn't a smart teen going to listen?

For Parents

Don't be fooled by the fact that your smart teen may be doing only mediocre work or doesn't seem to really care about anything. Percolating somewhere in her being is a clear, pure sense of what excellence looks like. What relationship do you yourself want to take to excellence? You might say to yourself, "Being a top ballerina is just too darn hard, and I don't want to support Mary's dream there," or "How many scientists really ever land on an amazing new theory? Isn't John just going to end up teaching everyday physics to bored undergraduates?"

That is, in your interactions with your teen, you might wind up trying to minimize the lure of excellence. Or on the other hand, you might support it, push your child to find the best teachers and tackle the hardest lessons, and live a life in pursuit of excellence. Each of these stances, and all of their hybrid permutations, come with real, life-determining consequences. You might end up with a brilliant, fulfilled concert cellist or a brilliant, miserable concert cellist—who in either case is living a life, ready or not, wedded to the idea of excellence.

For Teens

You have encountered some great things in your life: that great novel, that great film. It may have been something you yourself did: that one short story you whipped out for English class that was really good, or that time you solved a hard math problem in a startlingly original way. You know without giving it a second thought when something is excellent and when it is mediocre. And isn't excellence a lure? Can't you feel how you might just tumble onto the path of organizing your life around the idea of excellence? Or suffer some lifelong disappointment if you don't opt for excellence? Isn't it at once a lure, a trap, and the Holy Grail?

At this point in your life, you probably can't get a very clear picture of how you want to relate to excellence. Maybe you will revere it and love it but not personally pursue it. Maybe you'll consciously devalue it by announcing that the pursuit of service, activism, family, or something else is rather more important to you than the pursuit of excellence. Or maybe you will give your life to that pursuit and crave those twenty perfect pirouettes or that amazing scientific breakthrough. Can you decide about that now? Probably not. But you can put the following somewhere in your memory banks: You were born attuned to the concept of excellence. Like it or not, you are going to have to reckon with that lifelong attunement.

The First Signs of Difficulty

As a therapist and creativity coach, I've worked with countless smart, talented, creative adults who had very little to show for all of their potential. A common pattern emerged. From an early age, they believed in their ability and saw themselves destined to have a career as some sort of artist or intellectual. Brimming with ideas, they would start some project with enthusiasm—and quickly abandon it. Very quickly; one might even say, at the first signs of difficulty.

Rarely would it come to them to say, "I'm stopping because this feels too difficult." They had other ways of explaining their early abandonment. The project was too painful to work on. The project had no juice to it. The project had a plot hole in it the size of a flying saucer. The project too closely resembled something that already existed. The project straddled too many genres. And so on. Of course, each of these rationales might well have been a truthful part-explanation. But in larger measure, it seemed to be that the experience of difficulty produced sudden panic followed by uncontrollable flight.

The sequence we're examining in this section looks like this: enthusiasm, followed by the experience of difficulty, followed by some sudden, deep, painful doubt, followed by panic, followed by abandonment of your goal. This psychological dynamic plays such havoc in the lives of smart, creative folks of all ages!

Picture two divers: The first diver dives in and calmly holds his breath underwater, while the second diver instantly feels as if he is drowning. What is the difference between the diver who can stay under water for minutes and the diver who gasps for air immediately? The second is in a panic—but what is the source of that panic? A near-drowning experience? A lifetime of being told "You're no good at anything!" or telling himself, "You aren't very capable"? Who can say? What we can see clearly is a terrible problem: the way that perceived difficulty can instantly create a sense of panic.

Of course, the ensuing panic then makes you that much less capable. One of the tasks in Army basic training was entering a hut full of tear gas carrying, but not wearing, your gas mask. No soldier wanted to do that or thought, "What fun!" But the soldier who thought, "Okay, I can do this" found the task doable, while the soldier who thought "I can't do this!" and doubted his ability to tolerate a few seconds of tear gas would panic—and of course would then fumble with his gas mask, fail to get it on, and be forced to rush out of the hut choking and gagging. The panic made his fingers not work properly.

How is it that experiencing difficulty with one's work can produce such outsized panic? We're not talking about swimming underwater or tolerating tear gas, just having some troubles with the next sentence of your novel or some difficulty in dreaming up the next step in the theorem you're creating. Why does this feel so very dangerous? What we have is a great example of how our warning system against danger, our nervous system, which is what produces anxiety, can make bad mistakes.

It conflates troubles with the next sentence with disaster, with danger, with something outsized and terrible. No single artifact of evolution causes us more consternation or more pain than the way that our warning system turns a challenging moment with our novel into a confrontation with a tiger. The result of this "warning system misunderstanding" is that only a small percentage of smart adults are as productive as they would like to be or know that they could be.

Teens fall into a different category of effort, because they are not yet facing adult tasks like writing a dissertation or studying for the bar exam. Objectively speaking, their abandonments of tasks or goals matter less in the short run. But subjectively, just as much damage may be occurring.

The stakes may be different, but the dynamic is the same: enthusiasm, leading to doubt, then panic, followed by abandoning the project, resulting in a serious hit to one's self-esteem.

For Parents

You would naturally like your smart teen to follow through on the things that he or she begins, and it can prove highly frustrating to watch your child abandon things willy-nilly "without even trying." But it isn't that he isn't trying. Something else is going on, the "something" that we've been discussing, the way that difficulty produces panic.

How can you help? By sympathetically announcing that the projects we tackle can make us anxious the instant they feel difficult to us. That anxiety is natural and normal and does not signal disaster. Explain that coping with difficulty will prove to be not only a lifelong challenge, but his primary challenge, since as an intelligent young person, he is going to set himself demanding challenges that will require his being able to tolerate anxiety. He will want to do big things, and with that may come big anxiety. Help your smart teen to see that this is natural and even inevitable and nothing to panic about.

For Teens

What is your relationship to hard intellectual or creative work? Do you immediately provide yourself with an escape hatch—"Oh, that's a stupid assignment!" or "I'm not good enough to try that yet!" or "My drawing is so embarrassingly terrible!"—and stop? Or do you dive in, smiling as if you were made for the water?

The theme of this section is tolerating imperfection. You are not perfect—and you can't be. Your work is not perfect—and it can't be. You will experience successes and failures as a human being, and the work you create will run the gamut from terrible to excellent. Don't lose your chance to do excellent work by abandoning work the second that doubt creeps in or when you face some difficulty.

Difficulty is coming. Don't let that certainty put you in a panic. Don't let "I don't want to do that—that's too hard!" become "I will not do hard things." Have as your mantra, "I can see this through." Relax into the process, breathe, surrender, and accept. Hard things are hard, but don't turn that truth into so scary a thought that you send yourself into perpetual flight.

CHAPTER 4

SELF-CRITICISM

A Lifetime of Criticism

When she was five, one of our grandkids came home from kindergarten and told her mother that she was never again speaking to her best friend and that she was never again wearing the top that she had worn to school that day. "Why?" her mother asked. "Because Amelia said, 'Aren't you hot in that?' " our granddaughter replied.

When a child can take her friend saying, "Aren't you hot in that?" as a sufficient reason to end a friendship, we see how easily even the most idle of remarks can be received as criticism and how powerfully we can react to those perceived criticisms. And then when we are *actually* criticized—when, say, our teacher calls us out for not trying hard enough, or when we tyrannically criticize *ourselves*—it can be extraordinarily painful. This can happen, say, when we criticize ourselves for just missing violin practice (when all we really wanted to do was hang out at the beach). What does this all amount to? A lifetime of painful criticism.

If just once a day we either receive something external as criticism or we criticize ourselves, that's five thousand criticisms piled up by the beginning of our teen years. It is very easy to slide from all this—this criticism and self-criticism, as well as pestering and self-pestering that may become constant and chronic—to the belief that we are an abomination. Then we want to hide; we keep our head down; we slink around; we put on some weight to shield ourselves; we create an imaginary life where everything is much better; and we are sad, because who wants to be an abomination?

How much of the so-called "clinical depression" that many teens experience is exactly the accumulated sadness that has turned their indwelling into a perpetual winter?

What is so amazingly poignant about all this is that the criticism, actual or felt, can be objectively microscopic and nevertheless do tremendous damage. It can completely switch a smart teen's mind from her current heartfelt vision of the life she wants to lead and the career she wants to pursue to some other vision, one that has always been lurking in the background as the safer choice or "all that she can hope for."

That idle remark from her chemistry teacher might suddenly make her think that she doesn't have what it takes to be a doctor. That bit of rude, blistering pushback from the English department's resident grammarian, the one who never finds anyone's sentences adequate, could kill a teen's dream of being a writer. I know from forty years of working with therapy clients and coaching clients that these dream-killing events happen all the time. It is amazing the damage that criticism can do, even if it is delivered as nothing more than a raised eyebrow or an ironic smile.

For Parents

It is very difficult to keep from repeating criticisms like "You're getting crumbs everywhere!" or "Don't you own a comb?" or "Haven't started your homework yet?" You keep repeating these criticisms because you keep seeing those crumbs, that unkempt hair, or those unopened books. But while it is very difficult not to keep repeating those criticisms, it is not impossible to stop repeating them. They have become your habit—maybe your bad habit; and a habitual way of reacting can be changed if you're inclined to change it.

Does your teen really need more criticism? Think about it: Do you? Would you like to be criticized for all the things you could be criticized for? Wasn't the chicken you cooked a little dry the other day? Do you need someone to point that out? Did you become the concert pianist you always meant to become? Do you need someone to point out that you didn't? Did you lose something that you can't now find? Would you like someone to call you a "loser" because of that? There is no virtue or value in piling on criticism. That piling on is the easiest thing in the world to do—but that doesn't make it right.

For Teens

Here is a headline that you must keep front and center in your mindroom, maybe in bright red neon: Everyone has an opinion.

A given fact, say, for example, that you did poorly on a hard chemistry test, does not entitle your chemistry teacher to opine that you will never understand chemistry. And if he does assert such a judgment, that is *just his idle opinion*. Do not own that, do not take that in, do not turn that into jagged self-criticism, do not even hear it. Take it as rain pounding on the roof or as the cawing of crows rather than as words entitled to a place in your being. Those aren't entitled words, deserving of being taken seriously.

None of this is to say that you are exempt from scrutiny. You want to know when you've acted badly. You want to know when you aren't trying. You want to know when you've built a wall around you that maybe ought to have a door in it to let others in, and some windows to let in light and fresh air. But you do not need to hold that good understanding as self-criticism. That is awareness; that is honesty; but you do not need to put yourself in the docket and indict yourself.

Let's spend another moment on this challenge: to be real without being self-accusatory. It is that important.

The Road to Self-Indictment

Let's say you're seventeen, love literature, and read *Crime and Punishment*. Then you write your first novel. Will it read like *Crime and Punishment*? Will it make an impact? Not a chance.

No great writer, Dostoevsky included, has written a great novel at seventeen. But that literature-loving, excellence-loving seventeen-year-old, who may know intellectually that she is not supposed to be capable of writing *Crime and Punishment* at seventeen, is nevertheless going to feel disappointed by her first efforts—and perhaps worse than disappointed; maybe *much* worse.

Such inevitable outcomes, like not being able to write *Crime and Punishment* or compose a symphony like Beethoven's Ninth at age seventeen, do not *feel* inevitable. That seventeen-year-old feels she has some greatness in her, and when her efforts prove only mediocre, as they almost certainly will, she is likely, verging on a certainty, to blast herself, doubt herself, and maybe give up on herself.

During several of those growing years, a smart child will take his failures to heart—and there will be various failures. He will botch "who" for "whom" and "which" for "that" and feel like a grammatical idiot, even if in a corner of his mind he knows how trivial such a failing is. Seeing these shortfalls, parents are likely to react either critically or fearfully. They may demand that their child work harder or warn their child that their whole future depends on doing better. Rarely will a vigilant parent laugh these shortfalls off, fearing that freely pardoning mistakes, messes, and failures will "send the wrong message." Ah, but they aren't praising a mistake if and when they say to their teen, "You have great work ahead of you." No; rather, they are healing a wound and securing a better future for their teen.

By opting for this sort of response to shortfalls, parents aren't implying that mistakes are unimportant, that bad work is as good as good work, that not applying oneself is the road to success, or that giving up is admirable. Rather, they are saying over and over again, in as many heartfelt ways as they can muster, "Don't trash yourself over this misstep." They are saying, "Don't level some charge against yourself." They are inviting their teen to see the bigger picture, the true picture in which *Crime and Punishment* never gets written at seventeen and in which "that" for "which" is a minor and forgivable error.

Smart teens are peculiarly prone to self-indictment because they appreciate and revere excellence; they crave that excellence, want that excellence from their own efforts, know when they have missed the mark, and will give themselves demerits for those shortfalls. They may brush off that 60 percent on a French quiz ("Well, I didn't study!") or that C+ on a history paper ("The Napoleonic Wars? Are you kidding me?") and opt for studied nonchalance and irony. But you can bet that those demerits are accumulating internally.

This strange road to self-indictment is made stranger by a smart teen's need to assert her individuality. On the one hand, she wouldn't mind a good grade. But on the other hand, she wants to write her history paper "her way," maybe writing it as poetry rather than prose. Although she knows that gambit will negatively affect her grade, she does it anyway; she gets her C+ ("Interesting effort, but not the assignment!"), and then she indicts herself for that mediocre grade—even though she made her bed herself.

How odd that she should judge herself! It's as if seeing that demoralizing grade made her forget why she wrote her history paper in iambic pentameter in the first place. She not only chalks this up as a criticism but likely also as a warning about what will happen in life when she asserts her individuality. What are the two messages she receives from this experience? First, "I screwed this up." Second, "Being myself isn't going to play very well."

There are many variations on this theme. A smart teen heading down the road to unhealthy narcissism may turn all these perceived criticisms into judgments against the world and come away with a giant chip on his shoulder. A smart teen plagued by anxiety may end up with migraines and stomachaches. The self-judgment that flows from countless natural, predictable, and even necessary shortfalls can play itself out as everything from despair to grandiosity, from giving up to throwing up, from withdrawal into the shadows to a lifetime of irony.

For Parents

Remind your smart teen that he is not his products, outputs, or results. Great geniuses have received poor grades. The early efforts of the greats are routinely not great. Say to your teen, "It doesn't matter how good or bad the thing you're working on is. It really doesn't matter! Great work is ahead of you!" See if you can not only say this but mean it. You can temper this kindness with certain careful admonitions so as to ward off grandiosity, unhealthy narcissism, and the false idea that work isn't required for greatness. But start with the kindness. Every smart teen is on a slippery slope to self-indictment unless he comes to understand in a deep, visceral way that the quality of his early efforts does not matter. What matters is that he doesn't pass judgment on himself!

For Teens

I implore you not to get wrapped up in worries about how good or bad your output is. If the song you just wrote doesn't sound very original, maybe it isn't. So be it! The original songs are coming. If your history paper didn't sparkle, so be it! Your mature work will sparkle. If you only came in third in a national spelling bee, who cares? Your mature work will not revolve around spelling! If you have some natural talent for chess but also sometimes commit the most amazing blunders—so do world champions! If you can't quite grasp special relativity, well, one day you will; and if you never can, leave theoretical physics to someone else with "that sort" of mind and be brilliant in your own way.

Be gentle with yourself. Do not indict yourself. Un-justified indictments of that sort aren't fair, aren't nice, and aren't helpful.

Stubborn Defensiveness

Not so long ago, I had a first coaching session with a young man just out of his teens. He was a living embodiment of the themes we're discussing: high intelligence, a racing mind, a poignant grandiosity mixed up with massive self-doubt, high confusion about his career path, countless hours spent online daily, social isolation, a tense relationship with his parents, self-serving self-labeling ("Because of my ADHD, I can't possibly do what you suggest!"), deep sadness and self-loathing, and a stubborn refusal to let me get in a word edgewise ("I haven't finished making my point yet!")

He was in a bad way, which he knew. But like so many smart, fast, verbal, stubbornly self-protective young adults, he had to run his obstacle course his way, tripping and stumbling, doubting his methods, abilities, and mental balance, but adamant in his refusal to listen to advice or take seriously how low he had slid. He could feel everyone's worry; he could feel his own worry; but something in him made him respond to the world with, "I'm in terrible shape, but I'm fine, I'm fine!"

We only had that single session because I'd annoyed him by making observations and suggestions. Usually I work with coaching clients for a while, most often for a year or so. Then, typically, we'll take a break; and often the client will return, having lived more of her life and finding herself again in need of some guidance and support. But with a stubbornly defensive client, one who simultaneously has no answers and all the answers, whose modus operandi is to breathlessly speak without pausing so as to keep the listener at bay, one session is rather the norm.

This is a terrible problem. When a teen is desperately unhappy, sensitive to everything in his environment, bouncing from thought to thought, project to project, worry to worry, *and* adamantly and defensively walled off from help, who and what can help? A very practiced, wise, and warm helper can sometimes help; the chemicals that psychiatrists offer, because of their powerful effects, can sometimes help (and may also do harm); some great organizing task, like next year's major cello competition, may help in its way. But to the worried parent, it feels as if not even a mortar shell could penetrate the wall his teen has erected.

For Parents

It can prove maddeningly frustrating to see your smart teen so full of doubt, so self-destructive, so down on himself, and, for all that, so stubbornly attached to his own plan and his own counsel. You may know to a certainty that he is not doing well; you and he may even agree that he is not doing well, but his pressurized pushback is a rock-solid wall through which nothing you might suggest can penetrate.

What can you do? The world of psychiatry, to which your child might prove amenable, will typically offer one solution and one solution only: chemicals. A fierce debate rages as to whether those chemicals are ultimately helpful or harmful, whether they are actually "medication treating a disorder" or ought more properly to be construed as chemicals with powerful effects, or even whether psychiatry is actually a medical specialty. Those debates to one side, one thing a worried parent naturally thinks about providing her troubled, stubborn teen is what the mental health establishment is offering.

Then there is psychotherapy, which of course is just and exactly a kind of "expert talk." It is the quality, warmth, and compassion of the therapist, and not something magical or scientifically sound about therapy, which can (and regularly does) help. A wise, practiced therapist can listen—and listen, and listen—can interject at just the right moment, can dance that brilliant two-step of providing support but also demanding accountability, and can make an actual difference in your child's life. And, of course, an unfriendly or unskilled therapist may not help at all.

There are other resources, often scarce and/or expensive, ranging from residential programs to mentoring programs and from stress-reduction programs to wilderness camps, that may help. What can't hurt, of course, is your love and compassion and your steady availability, especially when your troubled teen makes some overture. Maybe he *finally* wants to not only race on, keeping everyone out, but also to listen. Life is a strange enough affair that even one such conversation might make a difference.

For Teens

It is imperative that you retain your individuality, chart your own course, and remain true to your values and principles.

But a defensive stubbornness that rejects all outside help won't really serve you as you try to make your way in life. It is one thing to be passionately adamant, and it is another thing to be defensively stubborn. Those two ways of being inevitably become intertwined and therefore need to be teased apart.

We have many reasons for wanting and needing to defend ourselves from painful truths. Maybe we've invested in the fantasy that we love Mary who sits across from us in biology class and we want to take her friendliness toward us as a sign that our love is reciprocated. But we know in our heart of hearts that she is friendly toward everyone and is just being everyday friendly toward us. Well, this is where our defenses come marching in. We may defend ourselves against that truth, that Mary is just being friendly, so that we can maintain the fantasy that she is attracted to us. When we want and need that fantasy, we wall off the truth.

My hope for you is that you can get familiar with your own defensive nature, see it for what it is, and learn how it operates, and then you will come to see how living defensively only *seems* to serve you. Yes, it may feel good to rationalize away your loneliness, displace your anger about your poor grades onto your parents, repress your truth about your sexual orientation, or proudly and stubbornly deny that you need help. But I think that you are smart enough to understand the downside of such defensiveness. If you would like some homework, you might read up on how defense mechanisms work. It's a fascinating subject, and a really important one.

CHAPTER 5

SADNESS

Existential Sadness

Smart teens are in grave danger of succumbing to a particular kind of sadness. It is a sadness that arises out of a too-keen understanding that human beings are merely excited matter, not put here for any purpose but simply arriving through various natural events that have stuck them on this planet for a certain amount of time, after which they will return to being blank stardust.

This truth about the facts of existence, that the universe has no purpose for us, no love for us, and no interest in us, translates in the soul of a smart, sensitive, idealistic teen into a despairing "Is this really all there is?" and a deep and abiding "Why bother?" Why run some rat race if at the end of that rat race is not cheese but death? Why write poetry to be read by three people who themselves will shortly cease to exist? Why bother to try to feed starving people when everyone is just coming and going? Just why even do it?

Billions of people have philosophical, religious, and superstitious ways of warding off the truth about our impending complete nonexistence. A smart teen, hoping against hope that she too may find something to embrace that takes the sting out of reality, may well dabble here and there, diving headlong into a month of Zen or a year of Kabbalah. But you will likely still have to color her blue. Even as she engages in wishful thinking about a loving universe or divine mysteries, her keen brain is saying, "Nope."

How can she not become genuinely and deeply dystopian? Of course, she will have her dreams, desires, ambitions, enthusiasms, pleasures, and all the rest. She can see herself writing novels; she can nurture that hope and bask in the light of that desire yet be existentially sad at the same time. Indeed, what smart adult isn't both at once, working at something, perhaps with enthusiasm, and sad at the same time? Isn't that the lot of first, a smart teen, and then a smart adult?

There is an unremarkable, not-quite-reassuring, not-quite-satisfying, but nevertheless pretty stalwart answer to this existential angst: to live. You take your time on earth as your time on earth, you don the mantle of meaning-maker and stand behind whatever you deem is important to stand behind, you name, identify, and self-select your life purposes, and you live, maybe still with some vestigial sadness, but maybe actually contentedly enough. That is the answer: But it is unlikely to be available to a smart teen buried in "Why bother?" She may not come upon that answer for another thirty years. That is a very long time to be sad.

For Parents

Over these many years, you may have quietly arrived at your own way of understanding the facts of existence, made your peace with life and with mortality, and achieved a kind of wisdom on these poignant scores. But can you remember what it was like being seventeen? That may not be possible. It may not be possible to perfectly remember that painful angst and sadness. But rest assured that you, too, had to live through seeing through the universe and staring at the void. That is probably where your teenager is directing her gaze today, at least for portions of her day.

Rather than try to sell her on the easy comforts of make-believe, you can smile and stare with her and exclaim,

"What a view!" Maybe she will shake her head; maybe she will laugh; maybe she will storm out of the room. But she will still have received the message you sent, that even after everything you have gone through, you are giving life a thumbs-up, not because it somehow deserves or demands it, but because that thumbs-up gesture matches how you have decided to live.

She may not fully understand your smile, your gesture, or your attitude, but she will have absorbed an important message between the lines: that a person can make it to your ripe age and still wear something like a smile. And if her sadness deepens, as it may, stop everything and have a walk and a talk, not about the pearly gates but about getting through this time of angst. What does she need? What can you do? Where might she turn? Be real and be a comfort. The void is very cold, and no one is properly dressed for it.

For Teens

There is a natural leap that you almost can't help but make from "The universe is pointless" to "What's the point?" But while that it is a natural leap, it is neither an inevitable leap nor the right one. The better leap to make is to leap right over nihilism and despair and land in the following place: "While the universe may be pointless, I can still make quite a good life for myself, and maybe for some others, too."

This landing place is not a denial of reality, it is itself completely real. It is you saying, "I get it, I'm not fooled by spiritually comforting ideas like Heaven and reincarnation and past lives and the stars aligning, but even so, I am going to earn some real comfort by looking reality in the eye, not blinking, and spending my time content to live creatively, ethically, purposefully, and passionately, which will be my version of 'I matter.'"

That is the place to land; where you do not gloss over the facts of existence, but you also do not mourn them. Instead, you smile—yes, perhaps a little ironically and sardonically— and make an amazing announcement that you get it and that you nevertheless intend to live. When all is said and done, existential sadness is a kind of petulance. It is you folding your arms and saying, "Damn you, universe, how dare you be so nothing!" Let me send you a wish: for less petulance and for all the courage required to create a life.

The Trouble with Nothingness

The French existential writer Jean-Paul Sartre, in trying to explain his concept of nothingness, argued that life is as much about what isn't there as about what is there. He gave as an example the following. Imagine that you are to meet your friend at a party. When you show up at the party, your friend isn't there. Isn't your experience of the party as much defined by him not being there as by who is there? Isn't it even completely defined by him not being there, to such an extent that you quickly leave in order to find him?

To a smart teen, this poignant, painful experience of nothingness might sound like, "This town has nothing to offer me" or "My family has nothing to offer me." If he is a privileged teen, he may have every one of his material needs met, from an en suite bathroom to a tennis coach to a stabled pony. And he may still experience his life as having a hole in it, the hole made by what is not there.

What "something" needs to be added to rid oneself of that feeling of nothingness? The right something. There is a puzzle, the felt experience of life, and there is the missing puzzle part, which must fit. If you are missing love, a cream donut will not fill that hole. If you are missing intellectual stimulation, a situation comedy will not fill that hole. If you are missing the sensation of speed, a sitting meditation will not fill that hole. In these instances, what you need is love, a great puzzle to solve, or a bicycle ride at a rapid velocity.

Ah, but how hard it is to know what is missing. In Sartre's example, it seems at first glance obvious what is missing. It is your friend, let's call him Joe. But is it that simple? Is it your friend that is missing and producing the feeling of nothingness? Or is it friendship? What if someone—let's call him Max—walked up to you at the party, began chatting with you, and you found him interesting? Would you still be missing Joe? Or would Max have filled that nothingness hole?

You can see what a difference it makes whether it is the one or the other. In the first instance, you go looking for Joe. In the second instance, you circulate and stand open to meeting a Max or a Jane. In the first instance, you stand bereft. In the second instance, you might even be enjoying yourself.

How are you to go about identifying what is missing? In school, you are offered classes with names like "calculus" and "Spanish." But you are not offered a class called "identifying the exact cause of your experience of nothingness." That is why school itself can feel meaningless, because what is absent—existential richness—may better define your experience of school than what is present. That you are not taught about existential holes is the hole in the program.

Consider some ordinary Sunday. You go over to your friend's house. He is playing a video game. How boring! You go over to another friend's house. She wants to show you pictures of her cat. How boring! You go over to another friend's house. He is mowing the lawn. How boring! You begin to want to pull your hair out. Can life really be this nothing? Nothing is going on anywhere! How galactically boring!

This puts you in a bit of frenzy and seems to pull from you the need for some crazy escapade. Can you see how the experience of nothingness can lead to all kinds of trouble? It can make you reckless. It can rule your life. All that nothing is really quite something.

For Parents

It is a natural consequence of being smart to feel that life is missing something. Your teen may respond to this felt sense of nothingness by sinking into a dark mood or by acting recklessly. It would be quite the astounding question to ask your brooding or acting-out teen, "What's missing?" What parent thinks to ask such a question? Nor is it likely that your teen will know how to respond. But maybe she'll have something to say, in which case that question could prove to be one brilliant conversation starter.

For Teens

Think about your own life. Is it more defined by what's missing than by what's present? If this idea strikes you as worth exploring, here are some prompts to help you explore.

1. Think about your own life. What important thing is missing? Does it have a name? Something like "adventure" or "love" or "creation" or "grandeur"? What is missing?
2. Are several things missing? Name them all.
3. If it's adventure, love, creation, or grandeur that is missing, what could help? What can fill an adventure gap, a love gap, and so on? What is the right something-ness to address your particular nothingness?
4. Might what's missing be the sort of thing that can only be addressed in the future? If, say, what is missing is an intimate encounter with thermodynamics and you need a ton of calculus first, what can you do as you wait for that encounter?
5. Can the hole be filled vicariously by reading, watching, or thinking, or can it only be filled by living? Is the only way to fill the hole made by your craving for Rome or an Arctic adventure getting on a plane or joining an expedition? Or can you bide your time by reading a mystery set in Rome or by watching a documentary on the training of huskies?

For the person intending to meet up with Joe, that party is defined by Joe's absence. Likewise, for you, life may be defined by what is missing. Joe is nowhere to be found. Is what you're missing anywhere to be found? And how will you go about looking for it? No one has yet dreamed up perfect answers to these questions. The challenge of nothingness is with us.

Dark Night of the Soul

A certain darkness attends the teenage years. In addition to existential sadness and the pain that comes with confronting the void, in addition to all the reasons a teen might have for feeling sad, from a difficult family life, to feelings of alienation and isolation, to a brooding worry about classes, grades, and all of that, there is an additional *something* that is probably best captured by the German word *weltschmerz*, whose simplest definition is "world weariness."

This world weariness, which feels like melancholy and looks like ennui, is a combination of sadness about both the facts of worldly existence, including the realities of pain, suffering, and injustice, and the facts of one's own existence, including a suddenly acute understanding of mortality and confusion and pessimism about belief itself. A teen pulls the covers over his head—really, over his heavy heart—and broods himself into the state we've come to call "the dark night of the soul."

Historically, the dark night of the soul has been associated with spiritual suffering, with years and even decades of painful uncertainty about the existence of God, the goodness of God, the reality of Heaven, and other religious doubts. As one tormented nun put it as she wrestled with her doubts about the existence of eternity, "If you only knew what darkness I am plunged into!" The eighteenth-century figure St. Paul of the Cross was reported to have endured his dark night of the soul for forty-five years. For the more contemporary St. Teresa of Calcutta, it lasted from 1948 almost until her death in 1997 with, according to her letters, only brief interludes of relief.

The secular version of this painful state is captured in F. Scott Fitzgerald's famous line, "In a real dark night of the soul, it is always three o'clock in the morning." Imagine if all of life felt as if it were those wee hours of the morning, flavored with insomnia and doubt; a smart teen may be experiencing life exactly like that. But how can someone so young possibly feel so world weary? Because, quite unseen, even by a smart teen herself, a certain collision is happening.

There is a growing but unconscious reckoning of the great divide between the world of fairy princesses and swashbuckling heroes, of Santa Claus and chocolate chip cookies and promises kept, and the muddy real world where famines and pandemics happen, where parents lose their credibility, where pursuits seem pointless, and where people are fitted with feet of clay. What is the sound of this angst? The heaviest of sighs.

This dark night of the soul is a decade-long first reckoning with reality. It is not the only reckoning, but it is the first and perhaps the most poignant one. And nature may require it. In some sense that is hard to define or describe, a teen is being tested by nature. It is as if evolution has decided that a youth must run a gauntlet from the ease of childhood to the strict requirements of adulthood. No painless transition will be permitted. Nature says, "I am giving you this heavy heart to carry—see if you can manage it."

Many teens can't. Their "dark night of the soul" experience joins with their other sources of despair to produce an extreme situation. If there were such a thing as a soul doctor, that would be the person to whom you would immediately send your teen. A teen in this extreme state needs a soul doctor, some combination of shaman, friend, and guide who can talk about this darkness in a way that your teen can hear. But where to find this person?

And can he even really help, if nature is demanding that every smart youth live through this on his or her own?

For Parents

For you, it may be 6 p.m., you've just gotten home, and now you're obliged to make dinner. And there is your teen, for whom it is not 6 p.m. but that "dark night of the soul" 3 a.m. Like Cher in *Moonstruck*, you may be seriously inclined to shout, "Get over it!" But where will that outburst get either of you?

Nor will it do to treat it ironically. The humorist Douglas Adams parodied the phrase "the dark night of the soul" in his book title *The Long Dark Tea-Time of the Soul*. But it is no joke to your teen, and it is no joke to you, either. Who knows, you may still be in your own dark night of the soul, it may be 3 a.m. for you, too, even as you defrost the chicken for dinner. No, irony won't do; you know better than that. But what to do?

You are obliged to wrack your brains and to turn to the help that is available for your teen, which nowadays will most likely be talk therapy and/or chemicals. We have nothing like vision quests or initiation rituals or evolved transition ceremonies to help with this prolonged period of heaviness. Maybe sharing your own "dark night of the soul" story might help the most. Because you did have such a period, yes? And maybe are still living it?

For Teens

Your "dark night of the soul" experience may not lead you to any epiphanies, awakenings, or reconciliations with the universe. It may simply be something you must endure, just as you must endure first loves and first breakups. But you do not have to endure it alone. Help yourself move from 3 a.m. to sunrise, when life seems possible again, livable once more, and even a touch magical, by speaking your truth to someone, even if that speaking makes you feel like crying.

It is of little comfort to be told to get help for something that has laid even saints low. But remember that love is coming into your life, and that will help. Engagement with the world is coming, and that will help. A lifting of this heaviness is almost surely coming, as nature doesn't really want it to last. This *weltschmerz* may not be easy to endure— but maybe the end result will be endurance.

CHAPTER 6

HUNGERS

The International Bohemian Highway

For thousands of years, outposts of civilization and culture have attracted smart, creative people, have drawn them magnetically to Athens or Constantinople or Rome.

For the last several hundred years, from the sixteenth century right up until our Internet days, outposts on the International Bohemian Highway have included almost obligatory stops in Paris, London, and Vienna, and in the twentieth century, New York, Berlin, Los Angeles, San Francisco and the world's other great meccas.

Not all of these stops were city stops. In one epoch, stops on the highway included the world's first libraries, often created and run by monks, and often on impregnable mountaintops. In another epoch, it included university towns, the Heidelbergs of the world. And always there were the specialty places, some entrenched and some pop-up, where like-minded creatives gathered, like Galway for traditional Irish music, Woodstock for a single game-changing concert, Costa Rica for an environmental pilgrimage, Tokyo for manga, or Buenos Aires for the tango.

The same people who needed an anti-fascist Berlin café needed a Woodstock in order to feel at home. These places were home. The International Bohemian Highway was a state of mind, but it was also a collection of literal places.

If you were a certain kind of teenager, you knew that you were supposed to live in Paris for a year. You knew that with or without actually knowing that. That dream circulated in your blood, pushing you to take (and mangle) French in high school, to read novels set in Paris, and to commune with the writings of French existential and postmodern writers.

This reality, that there is both a metaphoric and a real International Bohemian Highway, one that matters to smart teens and that tugs at their heartstrings, produces the following three enormous challenges.

First, there is the truth that nothing about being in the actual Paris, Los Angeles, or Berlin guarantees a good experience. Just read George Orwell's *Down and Out in London and Paris* to get a glimpse of how not okay a life of washing dishes is, even if you are washing them in the back kitchen of an elegant Paris bistro.

Real places are not necessarily inviting, embracing, or even interesting. You arrive in your so-often-dreamed-about Paris and it is raining, your room is damp, you know no one, and you don't know the language. Within hours of arriving, you have lost your love for the place—and maybe even your love for the underlying idea that you have a novel in you and that this is the life for you. This is a real danger: that stops along the International Bohemian Highway are wonderful in imagination but all too real in reality.

Second, you had likely anticipated that you would feel different and be different there, that you would be some sort of "new you" in Paris or Rome. What you discover is that you are still just you. You have brought your personality with you, the same personality that was having trouble writing that novel at home. This is a double disappointment, because not only are you left to deal with the same old you, but you now see that this really is you, that you are going to be this exact you wherever you go. There is no geographic salvation. This is quite a body blow, because you had been counting on change, on transformation, and all you have is more of you.

Third, if you happen not to find yourself on the International Bohemian Highway, if you find yourself instead in a dusty town or a suburban cul-de-sac, you will feel the absence of that highway. You will know, again perhaps without knowing it, that you are in the wrong place, that you are somehow lost, and that there is a "somewhere else" you are supposed to be. And so you will feel bereft. You will go through the motions of life because you must, but in an aching sort of way, nostalgic for a place that you have never visited and maybe have never even contemplated.

To summarize these three challenges: If you are not on the highway, you will miss it; if you do manage to get on the highway, it may not prove very romantic; and wherever you are, you will still be stuck being you.

But still, the International Bohemian Highway matters. It exists not because some planning committee dreamt it up, not because some mercantile enterprise thought it might prove profitable, and not because some geographer managed to connect Paris up with Berlin or New York up with San Francisco. It exists because inside of each of these smart, hungry pilgrims, this Highway beckons. Where else to honor their allegiance to truth, beauty, and goodness, to make their creative or intellectual mark, but in one of these sanctified places?

For Parents

What is your own relationship to the International Bohemian Highway? Have you traveled it, found it rutted, wanting, and ordinary—and maybe even dangerous? Perhaps you concluded it was dangerous, for instance, if it stole years and decades from you. Maybe you see it as the worst sort of mirage, a terrible chimera? Or maybe you meant to travel it, but never found the courage or the way to afford a ticket? Or possibly you are essentially antagonistic toward it, like that apocryphal farmer who wondered why anyone would pay more for a painting of his farm than for the farm itself, or perhaps this metaphor means nothing to you and has you scratching your head.

How you relate to this idea is bound to affect how you relate to your smart teen. Isn't your own relationship to the International Bohemian Highway bound to influence how encouraging and sympathetic you are or how discouraging and unsympathetic?

For Teens

I invite you to think about this idea of an International Bohemian Highway and about how it might influence your life, both for the better and for the worse. If you feel like doing a little writing, you might choose one of the following prompts:

1. Describe the International Bohemian Highway in your own words.
2. Each person has her own IBH, depending on her interests. Someone with a love of fashion might crave Paris, New York, and Milan, someone with a love of theater might crave New York and London, someone with a love of the bagpipes might crave certain musically rich villages in England, Scotland, and Ireland. Do you have your own particular IBH?

3. If you are "trapped" in a locale very far from the IBH, how will you manage? Do you have to physically leave, or are there other alternatives?
4. There is the romance of somewhere like Paris, and then there is the reality. How will you weigh the romance versus the reality? What are your thoughts on this important question?

Idealism

Intelligence allows for abstract thinking. "I want the banana muffin that's sitting there" is not an abstract thought. It is as concrete as concrete can be. "What is the fair distribution of that banana muffin?" is an abstract thought requiring the thinker to consider all sorts of things, many of them imponderable. Thinking about that might take her all the way to Marx and Lenin. "I want that banana muffin" is evolutionarily simple and exactly what we would expect our selfish genes to say. Bringing a word like "fair" into the mix leads to idealism, which, for a smart teen and the smart adult she becomes, will prove a lifelong challenge.

There is a direct connection between abstraction and idealism. When words like "fairness" and "justice" and "rights" and "equality" begin to percolate in a brain, it is a natural next step to think, "Yes, those are clearly righteous things," followed by, "And I am for them and want them." You might tell that smart teen, "Ah, that is so romantic, imagining that there could ever be justice!" or "Come on, don't be a fool, fairness is unrealistic and even un-American." But that teen will shake his head and reply, "Sorry, romantic or not, realistic or not, I've got to cast my vote for what's good."

Idealism is wonderful and terrible. It is wonderful when a human being decides to side with the good. But it is terrible how much pain can follow as one encounters the real world. There is the pain as one encounters unbending reality, and there is also pain as one encounters one's own conflicting needs and wants: the desire for justice competing with the desire for a house on the hill, the desire for freedom competing with the desire to fit in and get along, the desire for unselfishness competing with the desire to do selfish things. No human being is a selfless saint—and so inner conflicts rage.

And even if you aspire to be a selfless saint, ethics are complicated. Values and principles compete and collide. Will you volunteer to work for that pure like-minded candidate who has no chance of winning or the flawed like-minded candidate who can win? Will you betray your friend who has turned criminal? Will you go off to fight an anti-fascist war that you believe needs fighting when your ailing parents need you at home? Idealism is bound to smack up against such realities. What will you do?

It isn't that a smart teen is picturing utopia. Indeed, a dystopian vision of life may well make more sense to her. She may see very clearly that life is unfair. She is not picturing utopia, and she is not being unrealistic or overly romantic. She simply wants to stand up for the good. And that will not prove easy. She will want her car, even if riding a bicycle is environmentally purer. She will want bacon, even if she sympathizes with pigs. She will forget her ideals in the face of real-world blandishments. That is, she will be human; and her idealism will haunt her and never really leave her.

For Parents

What stance do you want to take with respect to your teen's idealism? Say that the following happens. Your teen comes home and announces that it is completely unfair that her math teacher always calls on the boys to answer his questions. She wants to mount a protest. You admire her values and pluck, but you also know that such a protest would likely (maybe even certainly) harm her in the long run, maybe in terms of her math grade or by her getting labeled a troublemaker, maybe in terms of college recommendations. How do you want to play this?

Take this matter a step further and think about your answer to the following question: "What is my fundamental stance with regard to my teen's idealism?" Is it clearly one thing? Is it clearly another thing? Is it necessarily contextual? Picture a variety of scenarios, from your smart teen wanting to volunteer for the equivalent of the Peace Corps to her wanting to become an inner-city public school teacher. What do you think? How do you feel?

Your smart teen may suddenly turn idealistic out of a clear blue sky because of a thought she's had or something she's encountered. Get ready for that vegan from nowhere, that pacifist who looks just like your daughter, that sudden environmental activist wearing the clothes of your son. He or she will be very adamant—and isn't that wonderful?

For Teens

We dearly need words like fairness, justice, and equality and phrases like human rights and civil rights to mean something to you. You are the next generation, the next round of human beings tasked with keeping freedom and civilization afloat. We must encourage your idealism and rein in our own cynicism and pessimism. But at the same time, we must warn you: Idealism is not easy.

Taking on teaching inner-city kids or defending the indigent is not a walk in the park. We can't in good conscience sell you on idealism without acknowledging its difficulty. It will be hard. The sharpies and realists will make the big bucks, live in the big houses, swim in the big pools, and laugh at your idiotic romanticism. Oh, they will let you play Don Quixote as long as you don't interfere in the slightest with their self-aggrandizing schemes. But if you do dare get in their way, watch out!

So don't be surprised if your parents find it hard to share your enthusiasm for inner-city teaching, public defending, civil rights advocacy, environmental activism, volunteering in Africa, or jousting with windmills. They want to share your enthusiasm—but they also want an easier life for you than one based on idealism. I want that easier life for you, too. But I also want and need your idealism. Of course, this issue may leave you in two minds. Really, how can it not?

Recognition

In our culture, coming in second for the senior English Award makes you a loser. If you're that second-place finisher, that's exactly how you'll feel. We're all conditioned to feel that way.

That's why so many smart teens refuse to compete or to seek out recognition. They are clear-eyed enough to know that the odds are against them winning, that winning is connected to popularity and other hellish considerations, and that the recognition available to them is hardly worth the effort. Given the long odds of winning something which may not amount to genuine recognition but just a victory of appearance over substance, many a smart teen will reply, "No, thank you."

But even as they refuse to play the recognition games available to them, they still crave that recognition. How can that craving be satisfied? A smart teen is likely to look that hard question straight in the eye, shake her head, and mournfully announce, "It's not going to happen."

Most smart teens will fall into this category. Some, however, will opt to compete for recognition. For them, their life may be organized around violin lessons, more violin lessons, recitals, scholarship offers to a conservatory, and dreams of a career as a soloist, or else chess study, more chess study, a million chess games against computers and humans, a climbing chess ranking, a state championship title, a national title, and a shot at the world championship, or angling to solve the greatest math puzzle they can find (maybe the 3X + 1 puzzle that has driven many mathematicians mad) so as to get their name attached to its solution for all eternity.

We have two groups, then: those who will refuse to compete and those who will compete. But probably the largest group by far is a third group who ride the rollercoaster of sometimes competing and rather more often not competing. Their craving for recognition propels them to enter the science fair; their entry is decent but not earth-shaking; they do not win, and they do not enter the next year. Or they play in one chess tournament, do middling well, and win one interesting game, but then they get trounced by the school's best player and do not enter any more chess tournaments. Or they go out for the school play, fancying themselves perfect for the brooding main character (given how much they brood), get a bit part instead, soldier their way through the run of the play, and never audition again.

Complicating matters is the truth that not all recognition is psychologically equal. Getting an A when half the class gets As won't feel like real praise. But having someone you admire read one of your poems and respond with, "You are a real poet," will not only make your day but may make your life. One such moment of recognition, even as brief as five words of heartfelt praise, has sent many a smart teen in a lifelong direction. This is its own danger: when one craves recognition so much, getting it may prove a fantastically outsized moment, one that changes everything.

For Parents

It may be hard to believe that your slouchy, silent, morose teenager is craving recognition. But he may in his slouchy, silent, morose way be craving nothing less. Has he earned it by virtue of dropping his dirty clothes on the floor or by leaving the refrigerator door open for the billionth time? He has not. But you might nevertheless find it in your heart to recognize his essential wonderfulness by spontaneously saying "You are the greatest!" or by remarking out of the blue, "I see you are going far!" These may sound like absurd and quite unearned commendations to bestow upon your slouchy, silent, morose teenager. But if you let them come from your heart and not your head, it'll be easy to speak to them.

Once upon a time, you could say to your five-year-old "That's great!" about just about anything she brought home from kindergarten. You could provide her with some over-the-top, enthusiastic recognition for the smallest feat, from spelling her name with all the letters in the right order to making a paper airplane that almost flew. Not so with your sixteen-year-old. Now your interactions are likely glancing and tense, having to do with a million "shoulds."

Therefore, life with your teen is going to present you with precious few opportunities to recognize her in the manner she craves. So, you will have to create those opportunities out of thin air. Create one today, and another on Friday, and maybe one next Tuesday. A few fine words, a smile, a hug— that is your Nobel Prize for her. And you know what? She will prize it.

For Teens

It is fine to want to win a Nobel Prize and be recognized by all the world for your brilliance and your accomplishments. To crave such accolades connects to your desire to manifest your human potential and to do excellent work. This urge arises because you have passion, curiosity, life energy, ambitions, and the sense that you and your efforts matter. These are good things! But I'm also sure that you recognize the extent to which the craving to be recognized is a trap. How wide it can open the door to disappointment and sadness!

What to do? Refuse to want that recognition? Reject that pulsating hunger as unseemly, as a feature of your grandiosity and your unhealthy narcissism? Or embrace it and risk huge defeats and a world of pain? Okay. Let's take a breath. Slow down now. Let's think about this calmly. Remember that you are exactly where you are, not apportioning a hundred-million-dollar movie budget or racing to create a life-saving vaccine. You are caught in your teenage years. Given where you find yourself, by all means want the recognition that you want. But be easy with the truth that, odds are, it must come later.

Maybe you will prove the exception and solve a great math puzzle at the age of sixteen or be invited to solo with the Vienna Philharmonic at the age of eighteen. But, more likely, your time must come later. Want what you want—that is just fine. But find some deep reservoir of patience. The recognition that you crave is still rather far off in the distance.

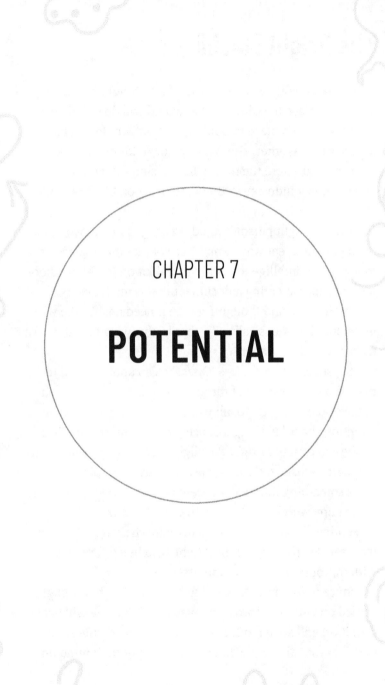

CHAPTER 7

POTENTIAL

The Bright Flashlight

Imagine that you had a very powerful flashlight but had no particular place to point it. What would you do? Well, you might hunt for a place to point it, but that would feel like a very artificial enterprise. What you would probably do is shrug, make sure the flashlight was shut off, and put it away. And wouldn't everything seem a good bit darker and gloomier then?

Until a bright person's mind is engaged in real work, he or she has no great way to make use of that intelligence or to apply that intelligence. She can train it on her high school history paper, creating a document that is ten times more comprehensive and thoughtful than it need be, but she will understand how basically silly that is, throwing herself into a mere high school paper.

So, she has two choices. One, she can apply herself to that paper for the sake of the grade and the game and so as to have something to do, all while shaking her head at the attention she is lavishing on such a trivial enterprise. That is, she can turn her bright flashlight on the Thirty Years War and write a dissertation. Or she can refuse to apply herself, write something minimally decent or even shoddy, and end up grumpy with herself and with school and with life for presenting her with such an inadequate challenge. She can morosely keep her bright flashlight switched off, no happier with this option than with the first one.

Since it does not feel good to have that bright flashlight turned on with no appropriate place to aim it, she will likely turn it off and keep it off. She will then likely do the sorts of things that all people do nowadays to put their mind on pause: She will watch a show, surf the net, tumble into some social media rabbit hole, fantasize, or get into mischief. She knows that these activities do not hold great value *except* the value that she does not have to worry about where to train her intelligence while doing them. Rather than trouble herself about what to think about, she opts for not thinking.

An adult immersed in a profession can train her bright flashlight on her real work. She can spend long hours and full days moving figurative painting forward or researching mysteries at the cellular level. Since a smart teen is not yet in her profession, likely doesn't know what that real work is going to be, and may not yet have even a glimmer of what it might be, she is essentially bereft—and aware that she is so. She knows that "out there" people are writing novels and creating vaccines while she is just and exactly in high school. She knows this and sinks a little deeper into the sofa.

For Parents

It would be natural if you were holding a certain hope in mind for your teen. It's likely that you hope that he will do well at school, go off to college, enter a solid profession, and have a good life. At the same time, looking at your teen and seeing him struggling—seeing him angry, or friendless, or eccentric, or anxious, or weird, or sad—it would be natural if you were deeply worried about his chances of moving easily from milestone to milestone along some simple, happy path to adulthood. When you look at your child, you may feel your hopes crashing.

But it may be the case that what is essentially going on is that he has turned his bright flashlight off and that what he needs is a good reason to turn it on. Maybe you can provide him with that good reason, say, by pointing him in the direction of a vector calculus course offered at your local science museum, or by wondering aloud, "Maybe you'd like to learn the ins and outs of getting a rocket ship to Mars?" Or sending him the link to some summer expedition gearing up to find the missing link in Peru, with your amazing offer to pay his way. Or...

Of course, your teen may not take to this opportunity to encounter a little vector calculus. He may not be ready for hard work. He may not want to really challenge himself. He may not have the skill set necessary to make sense of the tasks put before him. He may be leading with irony and indifference and prefer to keep wearing those masks. He may be too demoralized to drag himself to the work or too disorganized to concentrate. In short, this gambit may not work. But it just might. It just might be the case that what your teen needs is the opportunity to shine his bright flashlight in the direction of something interesting. Wouldn't setting up that opportunity be worth the gamble?

For Teens

It is completely understandable if you feel that you currently have no particular place to apply your intelligence. A spelling bee? Hardly! Acing an exam? Who cares. The school debate team? Please! So, you are left shambling along, too disengaged for your own good, with a mind that may be racing but to no good purpose.

We have to watch out for that mind, mustn't we? You can't really just turn off your bright flashlight without risking your mind either spinning off into fantasyland, relentlessly pestering you with doubts and recriminations, or catching you up in some other unproductive obsession. Turn that bright flashlight off, and you may end up someplace unpleasant or dangerous. So, what might you do?

Find something that interests you and study it on your own. Immerse yourself. Read all the books of your favorite author. Journey with Newton as he lands on a new way to calculate pi. Trace the history of humankind by virtually touring the British Museum. Build your first online business. Digitally create a city of the future. Study history and learn for yourself what, if anything, can nip fascism in the bud. Really learn how a cell works. Turn on your bright flashlight and point it somewhere interesting. If you don't, who knows what dark places your mind may take you?

Hidden Under a Bushel

Many smart teens don't quite know how smart they are. As a result, their brightness is hidden under a bushel, hidden from others but also hidden from themselves.

This failure to recognize their own brightness can result from all sorts of causes. It might have to do with trouble with a particular subject, like math, which can be extrapolated into a general self-indictment ("I am *so* stupid!"). Sometimes a quite smart person simply doesn't get what's going on in a particular intellectual domain—for example, he just can't quite grasp the very arcane relationships between time and gravity. Throwing up his hands, he indicts himself as generally stupid, when in fact he is not.

Or this failure to recognize his own smarts might originate with family rules against self-praise and self-congratulation which make it hard for a teen to say, "You know, I am pretty cool!" Or it might result from immersion in a high-achievement environment, where everyone is preening and singing their own praises and seeming so very smart (whether or not they actually are). If everyone around her is using big words because they grew up in a vocabulary-rich environment, a smart teen might not notice that her talkative peers aren't really saying all that much.

Or this inability to perceive his own intelligence might arise in the opposite kind of environment, where if a teen is trapped among dull, anti-intellectual people, he just can't picture himself as smart. Not only has he no opportunities to shine, he may not even know what shining looks like. Imagine if a youth had never seen or heard of a book, or if books had been withheld from him. In fact, much of society is like that, purposefully and staunchly anti-intellectual. A teen growing up in such an environment might have no picture of what smart looks like and no sense of his own mettle.

Thus, it is completely possible for a smart teen to never fully realize that he or she is smart. This can lead to lowered expectations, with the teen choosing a profession a step or two or three below where he or she might otherwise have landed, problems with self-confidence and self-esteem, and a cultivated antagonism to intellectual pursuits. Not only is he not aware of his own intelligence, he may even actively dislike smart people and smart things.

Does this teen still possess the potential to be her smartest self? No one knows the answer; and while we would love the answer to be yes, all we can do is speculate. But we do have some clues. In the heyday of IQ tests, back in the 1940s and the 1950s, many interesting studies were conducted to see if "enrichment"—for example, providing "underprivileged" kids with books—would make a significant positive difference on IQ scores. The results? The IQ scores of the children who received no particular enrichment remained steady and the IQ scores of the children who received enrichment increased significantly. This is not proof positive that smartness can be upped or reclaimed, but it is encouraging.

It might seem that this isn't exactly a challenge, since if a smart teen never discovers that he is smart, then he hasn't been stressing or making himself ill about that; and maybe he might even be considered lucky since he won't have to deal with the many pressing challenges we've been discussing. This might be a case of let sleeping dogs lie, mightn't it? Except that he probably has some suspicions. Lurking in a corner of consciousness is likely the bothersome wonder, "Is this really all I'm supposed to be thinking about—how to stock produce in a warehouse?"

Indeed, that exact wondering may be why you are reading this book. You may be reading it to see if you recognize yourself. My hunch is that you do. If you do, then you have your own smarts to reclaim. That sounds like a tall order, and of course it is. But it also has a ring to it, doesn't it? "I believe that I'm actually smart—now, what do I do with that information?" What do you think?

For Parents

It may not be your habit to say to your smart teen, "You know, you are really very smart." That may go against some principle you hold about the virtue of not bragging. Maybe you fear you'll give your teen a swelled head. Maybe your worry is that he will equate "smart" with "not needing to work hard at things" and become lazy. Maybe—yes, this can happen—you envy his smartness, and rather than acknowledging it, you find opportunities to put him down ("Well, that was pretty stupid!"). For all sorts of reasons, you may be refusing to acknowledge and honor that your child is smart, and as a result, he may not know that he is.

Do you want your child's light to be hidden under a bushel? You may have your reasons for lobbying against intellectual pursuits, for holding smart people in contempt, for believing that thinking leads to doubt and that doubt is not acceptable. All I can do is ask you to reconsider. It isn't so much that your child has a "gift" that ought to be nurtured. Rather, it's that his heart is going to be hurt if he never becomes his full self. See if you can say those magic words: "You know, you are really very smart." Wouldn't it be lovely to see him smile?

For Teens

If you suspect that you are smart but have never let yourself say so and have never let yourself do the sorts of things that would require intellectual power, this might be a lovely moment to no longer doubt your own inheritance and to step up to the plate as a thinking person.

Trying to do this may confuse you. You may hear yourself say, "Okay, so what am I supposed to be smart *about*?" It may make you highly anxious. It may bring up sadness as you ponder how you missed the boat all these years, keeping your light hidden, not even knowing that you had a light to shine.

Yes, this announcement is likely to bring difficulty, not ease. But it hasn't been easy up till now either, has it? Isn't this the better difficulty, to embrace that you are smart and to live with the consequences?

Forced Modesty

One smart teen, perhaps one who is privileged and belongs to the ruling class, may lord it over others and tread arrogantly through life. In fact, this may be the picture most folks hold of smart teens: that they are arrogant, grandiose, smart-alecky, narcissistic, and immodest.

But there are also many very modest smart teens, some of whom are shy by nature, made anxious by the spotlight, or arrive at this modesty as a principled decision. Then there are others, an equally large group, for whom intellectual modesty is a forced requirement of their environment.

In the last section, we discussed the possibility that a smart teen might not know that he is smart (though he likely has some suspicions). Here, we are chatting about a different phenomenon, where a smart teen knows that she is smart but is forced to hide her smarts and to even suspend thinking altogether.

There is the modesty that arises out of shyness or social anxiety. There is the modesty arrived at through a wise and mature understanding of how one wants to present oneself. Then there is the unfortunate modesty that is the result of oppression.

Is a given teen wearing her modesty of her own accord, or has it been imposed upon her by family rules or social pressures? For this second teen, it is unlikely that her forced modesty is serving her very well or that she is feeling very happy. This forced modesty may keep her safe—but at what cost?

Where is all this oppression of the intellect coming from? One typical place is from religion. As a rule, intellectual modesty is seen as a great virtue by religion—naturally so, as a penetrating intellect would see through the constructs and contradictions of religion and an outspoken intellect would make those revelations public.

A particular version of the religious commandment to be intellectually modest is the following: that you can be as smart as you like, just as long as it is in God's service. As one cleric put it, "Intellectual modesty is about using our intellect to faithfully stir the minds of our youth to better see the beauty and credibility of the gospel of Christ Jesus. Intellectual modesty is about knowing what we can know, being aware of the limits of our knowledge, and always seeking to improve our understanding in pursuit of intellectual faithfulness to Jesus."

This socially sanctioned, forced intellectual modesty turns a smart teen's natural smarts into either locked-up potential or into sophistry, where he gets to make use of his smarts but only in the service of apologetics. He can argue as brilliantly as he likes about some Jesuitical or Talmudic opinion; in fact, he is encouraged to do exactly that—but he has no permission to think outside the box of his religion. If he did venture there and move out of the box, he might well enter that "dark night of the soul" we chatted about previously.

For a given smart teen, the constraints may prove very subtle. It may be simply that her family never holds intellectual conversations, and that while she has never been told that such conversations are forbidden, she has the sense that they would prove unseemly or improper. She knows without knowing how she knows it that if she dared to bring up Sartre on nothingness, Chomsky on late-stage capitalism, or Einstein on relativity, she would be mocked (or worse). So she doesn't.

How easily shyness, sensitivity, social anxiety, and forced modesty can come together to shrink a smart teen's vistas and prevent her from blossoming intellectually. This happens all too often and amounts to a cost we all have to pay in lost scientific formulas, vaccines, murals, and freedom.

For Parents

If you are the one forcing your teen to live an intellectually stifled life, it's unlikely that you're reading this book. So, let's say that you are not the culprit. Who is, then? If it's your sense that your teen is stifled in the way I'm describing, why do you suppose that's the case? Where would you point the finger? And, if you can see where to point it, will you?

Of course, this may be an inherited problem in a lineage. You may fall in a line that includes your smart teen but also includes you. Is it your sense that you, too, have been suppressing your intellectual curiosity, using only a portion of your brain power, and avoiding intellectual or creative work? Then perhaps you and your teen can step out together, out of the cave of constraint and into a vista wide, broad, and rather beautiful. Wouldn't that be something?

For Teens

The two questions for you to ask and answer are, "Are you being prevented from being smart?" and, "If you are, what are you going to do about it?"

As an initial foray into answering that first question, you might consider how much permission you have to think widely and broadly and to venture to hold any opinion, no matter how controversial. Do you have unlimited permission? Some permission? Very little permission? If the answer is only some or very little, where are the constraints coming from?

The exact location may be hard to identify, if, for instance, many forces in your environment are conspiring to limit you. Nevertheless, try to tease this apart. Who or what is doing the stifling? Is it a particular bullying parent? Your parents and your siblings, too? Your religious teachers? A mocking or caustic high school teacher? Your clique at school, who find thinking hilarious? Just about everyone?

What will you do? To move from forced intellectual modesty to bold intellectual curiosity is like embarking on a dangerous mission in enemy territory, even a life-and-death one. This is not hyperbole. In the history of human oppression, nothing stands out more than the way that free thought is punished. I am not inviting you to do a safe or a simple thing. You will have to determine for yourself if a given risk is just too risky. It may be—or it may be exactly the right next step in your personal liberation.

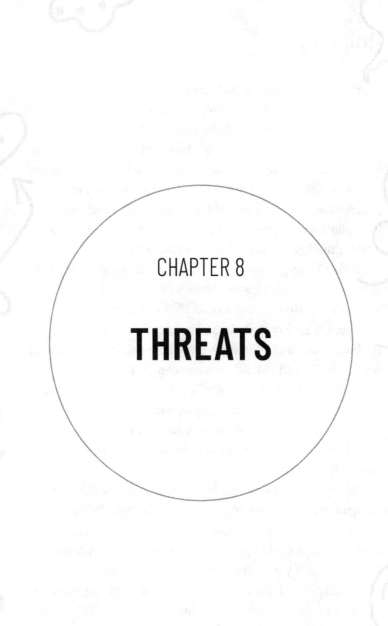

CHAPTER 8

THREATS

Bullying

Every movie of a certain sort has a scene where the nerd is bullied by the jock. Many movies have that as the movie's central theme, usually with the nerd and his sad sack friends ultimately getting their revenge. But as often as a smart teen is bullied in this way, much more often she is bullied in ways that flow from the authoritarian, anti-intellectual, anti-progressive, make-a-show-of-patriotism, join-us-or-we-will-hate-you nature of much of society. It isn't a particular jock who bullies her, it's her whole environment.

When I was growing up in Brooklyn, there was a legend spread by my Catholic school friends that when you talked back to a certain nun, she would whiz a spear by your ear. Presumably apocryphal, the story nevertheless seemed credible. It must of course have been the case that no student would be allowed to hold opinions contrary to gospel, whether that gospel was Catholic school gospel or Yeshiva gospel. Public school seemed, by contrast, a safe house, a place where you could be yourself and not be bullied into some belief about the infallibility of "our rabbi" or some man in Rome.

"Bully" is chief among a family of words that includes torment, tyrannize, oppress, persecute, intimidate, coerce, and harm. You are being bullied if you are knocked down the stairs or robbed of your lunch money; but you are also being bullied if your environment is so oppressive that you can't safely say, "I don't much care who wins the big game tomorrow," or "Gay rights are human rights," or "The earth is round." Every smart teen, whether or not she is taking some stand or voicing some opinion, knows intuitively when her environment is an oppressive one. She knows that there is danger around the corner, whether or not she decides to turn that corner.

A smart teen may find himself in such danger not just in the corridors of high school but anywhere. At eighteen, I found myself in basic training, where bullying was the order of the day, and at nineteen, I experienced serving as a soldier in Korea. I ended up in Army jobs, as a platoon sergeant and as a drill sergeant, where bullying was part of the job description. A smart teen will find himself up against both unsanctioned bullying—the archetypal jock and the archetypal nerd—and sanctioned bullying, where the system itself bullies. Even if he never has his path blocked by that archetypal jock, he will inevitably have it blocked by society. Society is the biggest bully around; and it always has its sights set on intelligence.

A smart teen will be challenged in this ongoing, enduring way by a society that despises intelligence, even as it sometimes may applaud it in a lukewarm manner. The jock blocking her way is one thing; society, in the form of school boards and legislatures and television programmers, is another. How are you supposed to handle bullying when it comes disguised as a fall season of one anti-intellectual television show after another or as a piece of legislation demanding that creationism be taught alongside science?

For Parents

A wise parent educates herself about the signs of bullying. Her teen may complain of frequent headaches or stomach aches, may fake illness, may suddenly skip meals, or may suddenly begin binge eating. Maybe he can't explain lost or destroyed books or electronics, maybe he's having nightmares, maybe his grades are declining and he seems to have lost all interest in schoolwork. Maybe he's avoiding social situations, or maybe he's arrived at the extreme of harming himself or talking about suicide. None of this may be caused by bullying—but it could be. A wise parent knows this, watches for this, and speaks up when she sees it.

You want to be alert to "ordinary" bullying. And you also want to be alert to that other sort of bullying, the bullying built into society because the majority of society's members resent intelligence. Whether that resentment has erupted or is only simmering beneath the surface, it is there and it is molten, your teen feels it, and your teen may actively fear it. What can you do to help her? Stand with her on the side of intelligence. Acknowledge the extent to which mainstream society may resent her, ridicule her, and bully her. Let her know that you understand her concerns and fears and her predicament.

For Teens

Hostility toward the smart is age-old and abiding. Let me share just one example, which isn't pure because it mixes up privilege with intelligence, but which is too striking not to share. The event known as the St. Scholastica Day Riot started on a certain day in February of 1355 when some students from the University of Oxford got into it with a local tavern keeper. This minor altercation opened the floodgates of resentment toward the University and its students and led to armed gangs arriving from the countryside to join with the townspeople in massacring sixty-three students and faculty (and, legend has it, scalping some of the victims).

We may not witness this brutal animosity playing itself out in such ways today. But we can feel it boiling right beneath the surface. It may seem odd to feel bullied when no one is literally bullying you, but that feeling is neither odd nor unjustified. That action of banning books two states away is aimed at you; the sometimes energetic efforts to kill off science are aimed at you; that political speech railing against "elites" is aimed at you. Your feeling is justified.

If you are being bullied, either by an individual or a group, get help. If, however, it is society itself that is bullying you, there is not quite any help for that. There you must take care, be smart, and resist as best you can. Society's bullies always come for the intellectuals first—that is one of history's clearest lessons. Your partially unformed fears are completely justified. But be brave and opt to number yourself among the resistance.

Labeling

If you are suffering from an illness, disease, or physical disorder, it is wonderful if your doctor can accurately diagnosis it and effectively treat it. That is the promise of medicine and often the reality of medicine.

But if you are not suffering from a disease, illness, or disorder and someone with power says that you are—labelling you in some way, calling that a diagnosis, and concluding that you should immediately start taking certain powerful chemicals as "treatment"—well, that is a very different story.

Today, everyone is under threat of this "mental disorder" labeling frenzy. A certain socially constructed way of looking at thoughts and behaviors—one created by psychiatry, supported by pharmaceutical companies, repeated thoughtlessly in the mass media, and used by virtually every mental health professional as a way to label and to collect insurance—is our current dominant paradigm. This fundamentally suspect way of doing things turns high energy into ADHD, stubborn individuality into ODD, despair into clinical depression, and just about any human thing you can name, from irritability to boredom to anger, into a "symptom" of a "mental disorder."

A smart teen is very much living under this threat. Put together restlessness, carelessness, forgetfulness, and fidgetiness—the very definition of a boy—and the mental health establishment is happy to hand a teen the label of ADHD for those behaviors. They would like you to believe that these ways of being constitute something called a "mental disorder" and that they know what is going on with and in a teen. But if you ask them directly, they will have to admit that they have no idea what is going on; and that their labeling guide, the Diagnostic and Statistical Manual of the American Psychiatric Association, doesn't even take a stab at naming what is going on.

Their labeling guide is silent on causes and silent on treatments, but they nevertheless want you to take it seriously. They want you to believe that they have done some real diagnosing in the twenty minutes they spent checking boxes off a checklist. They want you to further believe that the chemicals they would love to prescribe for a teen are "medication" chosen because they "treat" the thing they have just "diagnosed" as a "mental disorder." I hope you can see that there is a lot here to think about.

For Parents

Your teen may well be suffering. We've already looked at many sources of despair in a smart teen's life, and we've hardly scratched the surface so far. We have many more to discuss, from not feeling attractive to standing on the sidelines to receiving poor grades to collisions with family members. That is to say, your smart teen's despair is real. To make the unscientific and merely linguistic switch from this experience of despair to some medical-sounding condition that then calls for something called "medication" is illegitimate. But that's what will happen, isn't it?

Yes, those chemicals have real effects, and some of them may prove so-to-speak positive. They may flatten his mood so that he can no longer feel or drain him of energy so that he no longer fidgets. That is, they may do what they claim they are there to do: reduce so-called symptoms. And everyone, you and your teen included, may want that outcome and applaud that outcome, especially since the only other game in town appears to be mere talk, as in talk therapy. Why try to talk someone out of his despair when you have a powerful chemical handy? So, to repeat, everyone involved, including your smart teen, may want what is being offered: a label and chemicals.

Please educate yourself on this score. You may feel helpless and frustrated and have the suspicion that there are no really good answers to the question, "What can help my teen with her distress?" Naturally enough, you may then take what is on offer as maybe second-best but at least better than nothing. That decision is completely understandable. But do educate yourself as best you can as to what is on offer and what the alternatives may be. You may or may not opt to embrace the current paradigm, but at least you will have decided with your eyes wide open.

For Teens

I'm crediting you with being smart enough to understand the distinction between a label and a diagnosis, if you give yourself the time to think about that distinction. If an elephant is rushing at you, you can't know why it's rushing at you just by observing that it is coming fast. To assert that it has a "rage disorder" is just to affix a label to what you are observing. Maybe it just wants to get past you and play in the river. Maybe it is just stretching its legs. You can't know without knowing lots more, both about elephants generally and about this elephant in particular. And maybe you can't ever know—because really, how can you get in that elephant's head? If you don't know and maybe can't know, where would you get off "diagnosing" it?

Why is this important to you? Because the challenges that you face are quite likely to produce the kinds of difficulty and distress that nowadays get labeled with one or another "mental disorder" label. All of the following may then happen: You may think that you are broken; you may think that you have something for life ("Oh, I guess I'll always have ADHD"); you may be handed chemicals that, whatever their worth, may open the door to chemical dependency;

you may experience the people around you looking at you differently now that you've been "diagnosed;" and you may lose something of a golden opportunity to help yourself learn how to cope with life's struggles.

I am asking you to do some thinking, reading, and wondering. Educate yourself about how this pseudo-medical model of mental disorder diagnosis and treatment came to be, what it represents, which parts of it might serve you (and some parts may), and which parts might not. This will not be part of your high school curriculum, and you will need to do this research on your own. Educate yourself and see what you think. Please use your smarts to learn as much as you can about the current mental disorder paradigm.

Smart Teen, Powerful Addiction

The thing that we've come to name "addiction" is a powerful phenomenon. How powerful is the gravitational force that keeps the earth orbiting around the sun? How powerful is the force of a tsunami as it hits the shore? Addiction is like that. It grabs you by the throat and leads you around by the nose.

Why has evolution made us *this* susceptible to being hijacked by alcohol, nicotine, cocaine, gaming, sex, adrenaline, or designer brands? This is another one of those areas where we are completely entitled to ask of nature, "Couldn't you have done better?" Maybe nature had it in mind that the ability to productively obsess would produce inventions and masterpieces, forgetting how easy it might be for that same smart person to obsess about speed and vodka.

Since nature refuses to be interrogated, we will just never know the why of it.

The fact of the matter is that we are susceptible, and we really mustn't permit our naturally large appetite to transform itself into gluttony, our naturally high energy to turn us into adrenaline junkies, or our natural thrill-seeking desires to turn us to compulsive gambling. We mustn't let that happen. There will be abundant warning signs, some as subtle as changing friends so as to get closer to the users, some as clear as drinking bourbon in the morning. There will be signs—and a smart teen had better be watching.

Any teen is susceptible. But a smart teen is likely more susceptible by virtue of the constellation of original personality traits with which he comes into the world, which can amount to fertile ground for addiction. If a child comes into the world with high energy, a large appetite, existential restlessness, and a hunger to taste everything, how is that child not a candidate for addiction? In childhood, that may look like an obsession with sports facts or the exploits of superheroes. But as the years go by, those cravings change. One day, a smart teen might find himself much more interested in a pack of cigarettes than a pack of Batman cards.

If you add to this that a smart child is born with a broad hunger for meaning substitutes and quick anxiety fixes, deepening existential dread, and the special angst and despair that come with intelligence, you get a kind of recipe for addiction and for the related states known as craving, dependence, obsession, and compulsion.

Who wouldn't look to pills for help dealing with modern life? Indeed, it is commonplace nowadays for a smart teen to virtually demand a psychiatric diagnosis so as to get his hands on psychiatric chemicals. The pressure to addict oneself is everywhere, and the things to which one might addict oneself are legion. You—whether you are the parent or the teen—had better be watching!

For Parents

How can your lovely child have become an addict? It is just about incomprehensible. And yet, how close do each of us come to succumbing to powerful cravings that arise in us? Who might not find it easier to rely on the help of painkillers, inhibition relaxers, or endorphin releasers to meet the challenges of daily life? And if there is also some biological or genetic component, some particular susceptibilities or vulnerabilities, that would be influential, too, wouldn't it?

You must be watchful, which means that you must train yourself about what you are watching for. Are you catching your teen in lies that make no sense to you? Is your teen more secretive than you would expect an average secretive teenager to be? Has your teen's clique changed and moved in a direction that you maybe can't quite name, but that feels off? Is your teen stealing, keeping weird hours, or seeming devious? Chances are the signs will be obvious, if you have trained yourself to look.

And if you have your suspicions? Voice them. It will not pay to make accusations, but it will pay to communicate that you are confused and worried. Don't play cop, but don't play the fool, either. Lead with your heart and be the concerned parent. You are concerned, and you should be. There is a vast literature concerning addiction and recovery and innumerable resources available to you and your teen. Use all of that. Make no mistake about it: The threat is real.

For Teens

It won't do to have you pull out a ledger and list the pros and cons of drinking vodka in the morning or shuffling off to find pills for the weekend. It won't matter if the cons outweigh the pros by a ton. Such a reckoning won't lead you to conclude, "I get it, addiction is bad for me." Something very different from a balance sheet is needed.

In order to "just say no" to whatever substance or behavior may be threatening you, you must first "say yes" to a vision of yourself that refuses to include addiction. If you try to "just say no" into the void, the void will beckon you and seduce you. You need to take a step to the side of those incipient cravings or that already-in-place dependence and say, "I am not that person." Why do this? For the sake of your whole future and so that you get to live a life of purpose.

This stepping to the side wouldn't work if addiction was really a "disease." You can't just say, "No, thank you, cancer." It is customary nowadays to describe addiction as a "disease," but that metaphor is no more helpful than calling despair "clinical depression." Rather, think of it as a marriage made in hell between physical dependence and psychological dependence. The body wants what it wants; the mind wants what it wants; every cell, fiber, nerve, and muscle wants what it wants. This is a demand, not a disease; and since it is not a disease, the following is available to you: the logic and language of recovery.

Recovery is a beautiful word, a beautiful idea, and a beautiful reality. Millions of human beings have made the calculation that their addiction is not a good thing and that they are going do something about it, every day, in a disciplined and devoted way, because they do not want to be "that person"—an active addict. They may see themselves as someone who will always be under threat, not because they are weak but because life conspires to bring back their cravings. If that threat is forever, well, then, so be it—because you can meet that threat, every day, one day at a time, using your smarts to augment the solid ideas of recovery.

CHAPTER 9

ANXIETY

Sensitive to the Touch

Anxiety plagues just about everyone. We have a nervous system that evolution has created quite imperfectly, such that we are appropriately frightened by an approaching leopard and inappropriately (and quite outlandishly) frightened by having to stand up and address a group. We grow anxious by virtue of what is happening right now; we grow anxious thinking about the future; and we even grow anxious thinking about the past, as if the past could harm us in the present.

Nor is everyone sensitive to the same degree or in the same way. Some children seem to be born more sensitive, attuned even as infants to family squabbles, easy to startle, fast to cry, hard to put to sleep, always on the verge of some prickly reaction to what is happening around them. Others are made sensitive by family life and become chronically vigilant, constructing their life around harm mitigation and feeling nervous about just about everything, from the unseen, like germs, to the unknown, like life after death. Some people are born anxious, and some people become anxious; and, well, some are both.

What smart teen isn't highly sensitive? This high anxiety plays itself out in all sorts of ways, and one poignant way is in joylessness. When everything in a smart teen's life has the ability to produce anxiety, from tomorrow's test (and there is always another test coming) to her appearance (and a teen is always on display), how joyful can life feel? Anxiety and a persistent case of the blues are thus naturally connected because an anxious person is also not a happy person.

Another poignant source of anxiety for a smart teen is the feeling that he isn't smart *enough*, that other kids are quicker, more talented, and just downright smarter; and that they will get ahead and win life's races while he will topple down the ladder, all the way down to a low-paying job and a life of failure. Peter, a coaching client, explained:

> I know a lot about not being quite smart enough to do the intellectual work that you intend to do. I wasn't quite gifted in my IQ in junior high school. I didn't get accepted to a gifted arts program I applied for in high school. Although I made state band, got accolades for jazz band, was involved in my high school's honors theater society, and was a member of the National Honor Society, none of that felt good enough.
>
> I've had some successes, but just like in high school, what I achieve doesn't seem to be enough. I dwell on the things I can't accomplish, the negative feedback I've gotten. I have trouble focusing on any positive feedback I get. I' m letting this really take me down. Even to this day, as an adult, I mope on the couch in depression, and I'm anxious all the time.

Nor is this anxiety only about now. What teen isn't worried about her future, the future of democratic institutions, the future of the planet, and about all sorts of personal, global, and existential concerns? Like everyone, she will cycle from brooding about all that to pushing it to one side so as to get on with living. But how can those concerns not create a backdrop of anxiety and a case of the blues? The moodiness of the teen years is in part what is going on right now; but it is also in part about a grim-looking and scary-looking future. Isn't this a lot for a sensitive teen to contend with?

For Parents

Your smart teen is likely anxious a lot of the time. Be aware of this. Anxiety is no joke—you know that for yourself. It won't serve either of you if you try to make believe that your teen isn't experiencing anxiety when she is. Be real about it.

And try not to increase it with your own way of being. If you are going through life in a state of high anxiety, that's affecting those around you. Get calmer yourself. Yes, that is easier said than done. But if you want to help your smart teen with her anxiety, the starting place is to create a calmer environment, which if you are experiencing anxiety, means creating a calmer you.

Be real, be calm, and think twice about going down the route of supposing that your smart teen's anxiety is a "mental disorder" to be treated with chemicals. That path has a lifetime of consequences. I was on a coaching call the other day with a client who has been on an ever-changing cocktail of chemicals for going on fifty-five years—fifty-five years!

Be real, be calm, talk with your child, and refuse to rush down the path of "psychiatric diagnosis" without investigating the logic of construing high anxiety as a medical condition.

For Teens

If you feel anxious a lot of time, try to get clear on the better ways to manage anxiety and the worse ways to manage anxiety.

Worse ways are smoking cigarettes, drinking alcohol, popping pills, creating dramas for distraction's sake, defensively denying your feelings, continuing with activities that you do not really love and that make you too anxious (like competitive gymnastics or high-level violin performance), and employing sexual release as an anxiety management tool.

There are more: acting impulsively and recklessly so as to try to outrun your anxiety; managing your anxiety about your lack of control over your environment by stubbornly over-controlling what you can control, like your weight; dealing with your anxiety by trying not to feel anything, leading to you cutting yourself so that you again feel something. And there are many, many more.

The better ways are much fewer in number. Nature has provided us with a score of unfortunate anxiety management tactics for every fortunate one. But even if those fortunate ones are few in number, you can create a personal anxiety management program that suits you and that works for you. Your program might include a deep breathing technique, an anxiety-releasing dance, a calming guided visualization, a meditation practice, and a practice of carefully monitoring your thoughts where you replace thoughts that provoke anxiety with thoughts that serve you better. Will this do the trick? Don't you owe it to yourself to try and see?

Performance

Many teenagers feel as if they are always on display and always performing. What does this lead to? Massive performance anxiety.

Performing in public is among our species' most common phobias. Many of the world's greatest performers have experienced lifelong anxiety, and some have experienced it to such an extent that they could only record in the studio, never making public appearances, or could only get on stage with the help of chemicals.

If this level of anxiety can attack a masterful performer like Carly Simon or Luciano Pavarotti, performers who ought to feel pretty confident about their abilities and pretty immune to stage fright, how powerfully might it attack a smart teen whose confidence in his abilities, his looks, and just about everything else is likely far from rock solid?

How does this anxiety play itself out? A smart teen may not answer questions in class because even the thought of answering them and opening herself up to ridicule (or just scrutiny) provokes anxiety. She may not try out for band, a stage production, mock court, school elections, or any activity in the public sphere for the same reason. She may stay home on days when some sort of performance like an oral report in English or an oral test in Spanish is required of her. Or she may simply hide in plain sight with her head down and her stomach aching, feeling scrutinized and anxious all the time.

On the other hand, she may engage in all kinds of flamboyant excesses as a cover for her anxiety. Elton John, for one, confessed that he donned his most outlandish costumes out of a fear of appearing as himself and letting the world see the real him. This should alert us to the possibility that a smart teen may be dressing bizarrely and "over the top" not as a fashion statement or as an act of rebellion but so as to present a masked and costumed persona to the world.

Likewise, she may engage in risky behaviors like promiscuous, unprotected sex, or in classic anxiety-reduction activities like smoking cigarettes, drinking alcohol, or popping pills, to quell her anxious feelings. If a smart teen experiences her life as a performance, then she is making herself anxious at every turn—and all that anxiety will come with all kinds of potential consequences, from stomach aches and sick days to shows of bravado to secret cigarettes out by the school's back fence.

For Parents

You might be associating performance anxiety only with actual performances, like your teen's piano recital or gymnastics competition. You may not realize that she is experiencing everything as a performance, from entering church to shopping at the supermarket to getting out of the car each morning at school. She is likely chronically self-conscious, even if she is also bold and outspoken and otherwise confident seeming. That chronic self-consciousness is likely to produce chronic anxiety and the many effects of anxiety, from confusion to panics to agitation to sudden sweats.

The answer to dealing with the self-created anxiety that comes from experiencing life as performance is not anxiety medication. The better answers are to help your smart teen grow more comfortable in her own skin, to point her in the direction of anxiety reduction strategies—strategies that utilize tools and techniques like breathing, meditation, relaxation, disidentification, cognitive approaches, the physical and somatic realm, and so on—and to avoid creating yet more anxiety by not making a big deal out of small matters.

You may want to employ these better answers for yourself, too. It may not be just your teen who is experiencing life as performance. You may be as well. And if that's the case, you know how that feels and what problems that causes. There may be no better way to help your smart teen reduce her anxiety than by reducing your own anxiety. Anxiety is contagious. See if you can reduce yours.

For Teens

You do not need to see everything you do as a performance. Answering a question in class is not a performance unless you are thinking of it that way and experiencing it that way. Instead, picture it as something easy, straightforward, and uneventful. And if you freeze or stammer or lose the thread of your answer? Relax. Internally whisper, "Well, that was very human, wasn't it?" Refuse to allow that moment to injure your self-esteem. And raise your hand at the next opportunity.

Try the following mind experiment. Picture yourself playing your instrument, if you play one. Picture how it feels: Perhaps there is some anxiety, as we are always judging ourselves. But not so much, I hope. Then picture yourself waiting in the wings, about to play your instrument in a big end-of-year performance. Hear the audience arriving. Feel the difference? Some anxiety in the first case—massive anxiety in the second case. And all you did was *imagine* these situations!

That is how the mind produces anxiety. All that happened just now was that you *imagined* something—and still your palms may have gotten sweaty or your stomach may have turned over. That's how the mind's warning system against danger works, the instant it designates something as "an important performance." The mind can interpret "important performance" as something almost life-threatening.

See if you can cleverly slip "performance" out of your vocabulary. Begin to fail to recognize what the word means. You are simply getting to your next class—you are not "performing your way down the corridor." You are simply visiting with your friends—you are not "putting on a performance" for them. You want to talk to that attractive boy or girl? Frame it as "I'm saying hello" rather than "I've got to put on a show." It is our own unfortunate doing that we turn everyday moments into performances. We do that to ourselves. And by making that cognitive mistake, we increase our anxiety levels dramatically.

More being, less performing: If you feel that you are on display, that is you feeling that way. It is not the world seeing you as a spectacle. Have a chat with yourself and try to put all that unnecessary performing in your rearview mirror.

God-Bug Anxiety

It is customary for a smart teen to be pestered by two contradictory ideas: first, that he is as special a creature as nature has yet produced; and second, that he's not very special at all, just some excited matter burdened with pimples and bad hair.

This first feeling inflates him and makes him want to puff out his chest. The second feeling makes him want to crawl into a hole. Let us dub this a so to speak "god-bug syndrome," one that fills a smart teen with anxiety as he tries to make sense of—and live with—these two polar opposite feelings.

What does this look like in real life? Jonathan, a computer engineer and coaching client, explained:

> I grew up knowing that I could really do math. I had that kind of mind. That was clear to me from a very early age. I could do any sort of computational problem in my mind faster and better than anyone else. I was proud of that ability and pretty puffed up about it. At the same time, I had zero common sense or attunement to what was going on around me. My parents could keep any secret from me they wanted—I was just completely unaware. You could easily have sold me the Brooklyn Bridge. And I knew that about myself exactly as well as I knew that I could compute. So, both powerful feelings built up in me, that I was singular and great and that I was also wretched, embarrassingly naïve, and somehow unlovable because of my awkwardness and unmanliness.
>
> I remember making lists of how I could be more like a man or acquire more common sense or be more aware of my surroundings. It was pathetic. I was pathetic. My clothes were ridiculous. The way I wore my hair was ridiculous. But I was a whiz in

school, won everything that could be won, and was on my way to some high-paying computer job, or even loftier, some start-up idea that might make me billions. The kids around me sort of intuited that about me, that I was a pathetic loser who might also become a billionaire—and their employer. It was weird. I was both a pariah and put on a pedestal.

This cognitive dissonance produces a smart teen who looks confident one moment and ineffectual the next, motivated one moment and apathetic the next, sober and hardworking one moment and careless and self-indulgent the next. How can a person brim over with life energy and big plans one moment and feel so very down the next? He can cycle that way exactly because he is bombarded by two completely different messages, each of which has its reasons.

This god-bug syndrome has the potential to influence everything, including a smart teen's career choice. Sandra, a coaching client, explained:

> My parents always told me that I was very bright— that everyone in our family was very bright but that I shined the brightest. Maybe this ought to have pleased me, but I didn't really feel all that bright, not compared to the kids at school who were super-quick at math or super-quick at memorizing, and especially not compared to the geniuses I would read about both in school and in my spare time. I got a little obsessed with reading about all those geniuses because I had this powerful doubt that I was anything like them and I guess I wanted to confirm that to myself.

So I thought to myself, *where can you be smart, but you don't have to be really super-smart?* I decided that I would become a concert pianist. That sounded so cultured, and even if it wasn't the doctor or lawyer my parents wanted me to become, it was at least in a category of jobs where I'd associate with doctors and lawyers. I knew even then that I was making a very odd decision, one that had to do with feeling somewhat special but also not feeling special enough to try something amazing. So, I ended up choosing something that was perhaps the very hardest thing I could have chosen, especially hard because I didn't love practicing and I had performance anxiety. I think that if I hadn't gotten caught up in thinking so much about how smart I was or wasn't, I would have gone in a very different direction in life.

This epidemic feeling of greatness walking hand in hand with smallness plagues countless smart teens. It is rather easy to see how these two feelings might mutate into a superiority complex, a defense mechanism described by Alfred Adler where one puts on a grand show to mask deep feelings of inadequacy. A smart teen, feeling both smart and rather like a cockroach, trapped by his own shortcomings and by the very measliness of life, may put on that show—all the while experiencing high anxiety.

For Parents

You may have come to expect mood swings from your smart teen. But you may be less attuned to these other swings, from feelings of superiority to feelings of inferiority and back again.

When you think about it, however, I think you will recognize how this so-to-speak syndrome plays itself out in your teen's life, sometimes even in a single hour. One minute she is adamant about her opinion and certain that everyone around her is an idiot. The next minute she feels small, worthless, and pathetic. It is enough to make your head spin. It certainly is making hers do so.

How can you normalize life and communicate to her that she is not just one or the other, neither out-of-this-world great nor merely dirt? Give yourself that assignment. Think about how you might chat with your teen about that vast middle ground of excellence and failure, amazing work, and comic pratfalls. How might you walk that line so that you neither inflate her more nor deflate her while painting a realistic and encouraging picture? There's an assignment.

For Teens

Your brain can conceptualize ideas as abstract as the relationship between energy and matter; it can produce strings of words or of musical notes that evoke tremendous feeling; it can place itself in the vast universe and see itself living and dying. It can imagine, calculate, remember, and more. All that has to make it feel pretty darn special.

At the same time, your brain knows perfectly well all about its limitations, its absurd conceits, and its fleeting nature. Both are true; and it turns out there is actually no opposition. These opposite feelings are exactly what you would expect a creature like us to experience. Given the naturalness of this experience, isn't your job to live with it and to deal with it?

Laugh a little at your feelings of superiority—you are just human, after all, and not anything like a god. By the same token, refuse to turn your real or perceived shortcomings into anxious self-indictment. Forget about both heaven and hell and simply live with purpose here on earth.

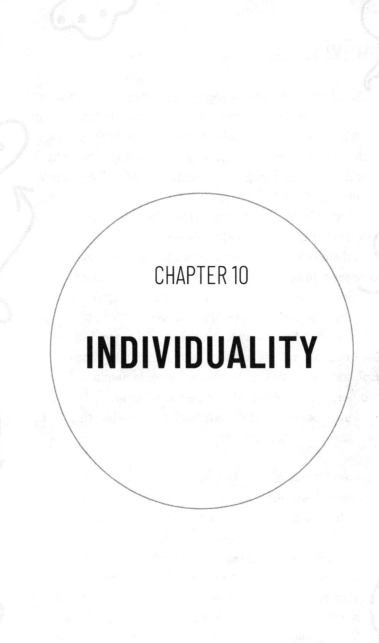

CHAPTER 10

INDIVIDUALITY

Individuality

Smart teens fall into two rough groups: those who assert their individuality and those who suppress their individuality. For both groups, individuality is an issue; for both groups, individuality is a challenge; and for both groups, the right balance between fitting in and being oneself is likely to prove chronically elusive.

Much of a smart teen's pain arises from this conflict between the demand to hide, a demand which may come from the outside or may be internalized, and the pressure to be seen, to be heard, and to stand up. It may take years, decades, or most of a lifetime to find the courage to stand up if the path has been one of suppression. It may take just as long to find a way to play along if the path has been one of defiance. For one smart teen, individuality may be aspirational, something he wishes he could manifest. For another, it may feel—and prove—more like an albatross.

Suppression of one's individuality sounds like this. Nina, a creativity coach, explained:

> I am forty-two years old, and it' s only been in the last few years that I came to understand my individuality. For many years, I tried to hide it. I knew inside that it was okay that each of us, including me, could do their own thing and be who they wanted to be. But in "real life," I didn't break society's rules, I didn't say what was on my mind, and I tried to be what was expected of me. My individuality was my secret, and it came out only in my writing.

My ideas, my thoughts, my way of seeing the world, they were all there, but I hid them because I had to deal with real life, with opinionated people, with beliefs and thoughts that were not mine. This process of allowing myself to be me is still going on, but I am no longer that child who felt weird in her own skin, who wrote in notebooks and never talked about her true feelings, or who chose to do what others think is best. Now I listen to me—although, if I am being honest, it is still a pretty mighty struggle.

By contrast, Andrea, also a coach, fought tooth and nail and every inch of the way to retain her individuality. She explained:

I've been fighting my whole life. In kindergarten, I wanted to wear the same dress every single day. Of course, my mother couldn't allow that, so we had a fight every single day—*every single day*. In high school, I naturally ran with the tattered jeans and no make-up crowd. Every day, my mother would say, "Andrea, why don't you wear something nice?" And every day I would storm out and slam the door. Was I doing battle with my mother? Yes—but not her, really, so much as what she represented: the reification of appearances, a smiling, fear-based life, something just plain false.

How did this work out for me? Not very well, of course. I put rebellion and experimentation on a pedestal and got into trouble with drugs, sex, and everything else. I had an abortion. I engaged in escapades that could have landed me in jail. I got terrible grades—well, decent grades, but just because I knew how to "cleverly" play the game. And I am still fighting, though the look of that is very different today. And I am still reeling from all of that fighting. Organizing my life around rebellion felt necessary, but I'm not sure that all that defiance has served me very well.

For Parents

You are of course smack in the middle of this issue. If your teen is dedicated to standing up for herself at all costs and asserting her individuality at every turn, you will bear the brunt of that. If, on the other hand, your teen is overly conforming and stuffing her true thoughts and her true feelings for the sake of getting along and not provoking drama or retaliation, you are likely part of the problem. If she feels that she must conform, it must be the case that in one way or another you are either promoting conformity or flat-out demanding it.

The twin questions a parent of a smart teen is obliged to address are "Can my child be herself?" and "How much can my child be herself?" I'm sure that deep down you agree that she ought to have permission to be herself. But you may have to bring that sense of acceptance into conscious awareness, because day in and day out you may be pressing her to conform. At the same time, you can't really stand idly by and let her do what you deem to be dangerous. Just as a smart teen must find her way between getting along and being herself, you must find your own way between those twin tensions. Will you let her be herself? Will you try to keep her safe? Yes to both, somehow.

For Teens

You had better be yourself. That's for sure. If you find yourself in a vortex of beliefs that you do not believe, pretending belief will harm you. That going along to get along may cost you the love of a same-sex partner, the chance to pursue a creative career, or the opportunity to escape your small—and small-minded—town. This may be the toughest battle you ever face, the battle to be yourself.

At the same time, you had better pick your battles carefully. If defiance is your way, there can be terrible consequences, from drunken car crashes to unwanted pregnancies to family estrangement. There is a cost to rebelling, just as there is a cost to conforming. In short, your choices will have consequences. This and this alone will make your teen years tempestuous, both with regard to what is outside, as you deal with life's rules, mean beliefs, and restrictions, and as to what is inside: your own confusion about how exactly to balance conformity and rebellion.

Loneliness

Picture a smart teen. She does her homework, maybe even with some enthusiasm, because she is used to doing a good job and getting praise for her work. No loneliness yet. Then, as a reward for finishing her homework expeditiously, she watches an episode of her favorite television series, an episode she's been saving for this Tuesday afternoon. No loneliness yet. Then she surfs the Internet for a bit, following up on a curiosity she had about what it would be like to live somewhere in the south of France. No loneliness yet. Then, all of a sudden, a feeling of intense loneliness comes over her. Where did that come from?

She was doing just fine, relishing her solitude, and then suddenly she wasn't. What just happened?

Loneliness is a message from the heart. It is the heart sending the mind a plaintive complaint, "We are not okay. We need other people. We need someone to love. We need someone to love us. We are aching." It is a tug from the heart on the whole being. A moment before, the heart was just beating. Then, out of the blue, it felt bereft, so it delivered its anguished message, a message that is received as loneliness.

This is complicated by the other themes and challenges we've been discussing. If, for instance, a smart teen is used to seeing through deceptions and doesn't really trust this species of ours, her heartfelt feeling of loneliness will likely collide with this counter feeling that people aren't to be trusted or aren't worth the bother. Likewise, if she doesn't really enjoy or respect her peers, and/or if she sees light chitchat among adults as inane, when she thinks about all that, it may strike her that solitude is preferable to what's available out there in terms of human contact. At once lonely and skeptical, she may write in her journal about the pain she is feeling rather than venture out to be with someone.

Further dampening her desire to do something about her loneliness is her need to protect her individuality. This sounds like, "Anybody I might be with would only reduce my freedom." Her quest to be herself and to remain herself butts heads with her desire for love, intimacy, friendship, warmth, and connection. She may not be conscious that she is protecting herself this way, but the thought is likely lurking somewhere in a corner of her consciousness.

The ideal to be hoped for is that a smart teen can relax her reluctance a little for the sake of the heart warmth that comes with sharing a bit of life with other human beings. And if she is lucky enough to land on this connection, that she finds one other warm heart, maybe a dear friend or an intimate companion, who supports her individuality, gives her comfort and freedom in equal measure, and in no way acts as an anchor or a drag. This ideal can be described—but can it be found in real life?

Maybe not, in part because the person a smart teen would be attracted to will likely be very much like herself, with his own self-protective need to guard his individuality. Both may be wary, prickly, and perhaps overly quick to dissolve whatever relationship they've formed. The first molehill of a disagreement may remind each of them how much they value their solitude, their independence, and the sanctity of their own path.

For most human beings, loneliness is on the menu. It is likely on the menu for the smart teens reading this book. But it is not something to "treat" or to "cure" or to simply endure. Warm connections can be made since hearts are built to mingle. It may take some time, maybe years or longer, to find the right balance between open-hearted intimacy and staunch independence. But what a discovery that will be!

For Parents

It may be clear to you that your smart teen is lonely. But it will hardly work to cheerfully suggest that he go out and be with his friends or somehow meet someone.

All of the following may get in the way of him making that effort: his shyness and sensitivities; his fear of performing poorly; his self-indictments and feelings of unworthiness; his preference for solitude; his skepticism about the value of relating; and the challenge we've been discussing, his perhaps unconscious worry that other people will deflect him from his path and reduce his freedom.

That is a lot, and some cheerful suggestion on your part is unlikely to make much of an impression. Something more useful to try might be a conversation about coldness and warmth, about the perils of icy seclusion and the sunniness of shared smiles and a little handholding. Maybe he won't be able to buy this vision right now, but you will have put a lovely picture in his head, one that may endure.

For Teens

You may think that it is somehow practical or wise to opt for loneliness, given both your misgivings about yourself and your misgivings about other people. But it isn't practical or wise. Loneliness is your heart aching, and loneliness has nothing to recommend it. Put your misgivings aside and announce, even if it is just in a whisper, "I want connection."

Be a friend; not a dishrag of a friend, not a second banana, not someone obsequious or dependent, and neither a boss nor a diva, but a warm-hearted equal, someone you would want as a friend. Be an attractive friend and attract someone to laugh with, to go to museums with, to discover a new star with. This is a dance—and you may not know how to dance. But wouldn't it be lovely to learn?

Guarding your independence, your individuality, and your right to travel your own path is a concern that is second to none. But don't travel that path encased in a block of ice. You can safely thaw a little. Give it a try!

Katya on Individuality

In this section, I wanted to share some of the thoughts and observations of a real live smart teen, my granddaughter Katya, who (as I write this) is eighteen. Katya was born and raised in Russia, primarily in the Siberian city of Omsk, speaking Russian and living a Russian life. Her experience is not that of an American teenager, and yet her concerns speak to the universality of the challenges we've been discussing. Here is Katya on individuality and on some of the other issues we've been discussing:

> One of my friends is bored by school. He wants to be an architect, and all day long he draws plans for buildings and makes projections of model cities. But it's complicated. On the one hand, he wants to build cities. On the other hand, he claims to dislike science and technology and even goes so far as to say that he can't understand geometry. I wonder if he is trying to protect himself and protect

his creativity by acting like he doesn't like certain things and that he can't do certain things. So, he jokes about his ability to concentrate, dresses oddly, and most of his classmates find him weird. To the world, he looks lazy, but I'm sure it's something else. He doesn't pay much attention to anything except his own drawings and doesn't seem to mind being isolated and something of an outcast.

Another friend also has a complicated story. From childhood, her mother told her that she was extremely bright and talented, which was true, and that she had huge potential and was superior to other people. At about the age of thirteen or fourteen, my friend started to become very difficult and very oppositional. She became a vegetarian, began to engage in free love, and started taking drugs (and was also a passionate volunteer!) Her mother, who had praised her so much, washed her hands of her and stopped supporting her financially and emotionally. Now she is in a technical school (called "college" here, which is lower than "university"), and not at all making use of her great potential.

Another friend is very bright and creative. He's a visual artist and a poet, he's interested in philosophy and nature, he reads widely and is especially interested in Japanese culture, and he smokes a lot of weed. His main challenge is that he rejects everyone's opinion, even those closest to him. His position seems to be "Nobody touches me, and I touch nobody." He can't tolerate criticism, and he refuses to believe that he is ever wrong. We did some artwork together and found the collaboration very successful, but our reactions to its reception were very different. I was afraid of the public reaction, while he was dismissive of it. I maybe let criticism in too easily, and maybe he defended himself from criticism too much.

In my own case, I have had my problems finding the recognition I crave. I never joined a group of friends and so never had the kind of recognition you get from being part of a group. I was always looking for just the right person to respond to my work and my thoughts, someone who respected me and whom I could respect. This may have been partly the case because I've always felt that I would be leaving this Russian environment to study elsewhere, many of my friends live in other countries, so maybe I've kept a certain distance all these years from my Russian peers. I've always been drawn to Italy, and that's where I'll go to university. And, of course, Covid played a part in all of this. I think that when I change the conditions of my life and begin my university life in Italy, I'll find the recognition I crave.

I have a younger friend who is a dancer. She is talented, passionate, and loves to shine, but she has a very complicated and difficult relationship with her primary trainer. My friend is naturally a free spirit and is not doing well being told what to eat, how to do her hair, how to look, and how to live her life. When it comes to dance instruction, she can listen; but when it comes to how she should live, there she feels that her freedom is being stolen. This has caused her to lose motivation. Her mother has tried to intervene with the primary trainer, but the trainer was quite manipulative, and the situation did not improve. Now my friend has to decide if she wants to continue with dance, which she loves, knowing that she is going to encounter more people along the way who are as controlling, critical, and manipulative as this trainer.

Speaking of dance, I use dance to help with my mood swings. Like most of my smart friends, who have many ups and downs even in a very short period of time, I experience a great many rapidly changing moods in a day. This affects everything we do, from our interpersonal relationships to our ability to create. To deal with these mood swings, I open my playlist, start to dance, and repeat certain words in a ritualistic way. It is sort of a ceremony for me; it liberates my emotions, and I feel calmer and better. I think this could work for other teens, too.

I think that all smart teens are looking for recognition and admiration. They are bothered by criticism and can even stop trying when they're criticized. For better or worse, they depend on the opinions of their peer group, and to gain recognition they can become flamboyant and engage in shocking activities so as to attract attention. This is all a learning process, but a *hard learning process because there are so many emotions, so much self-analysis and self-questioning, so much hunting for the truth and trying to make sense of the world, so much adrenaline-seeking, and so much stubbornness as we try to take a stand and do things our own way.*

My mother always says, "If you want to learn how to do something, do it. If you want to know how to drive a car, drive it. If you want to know how to speak a foreign language, learn it." Well, I wanted to contribute this chapter and I did it. ☺ I hope you've found my thoughts valuable.

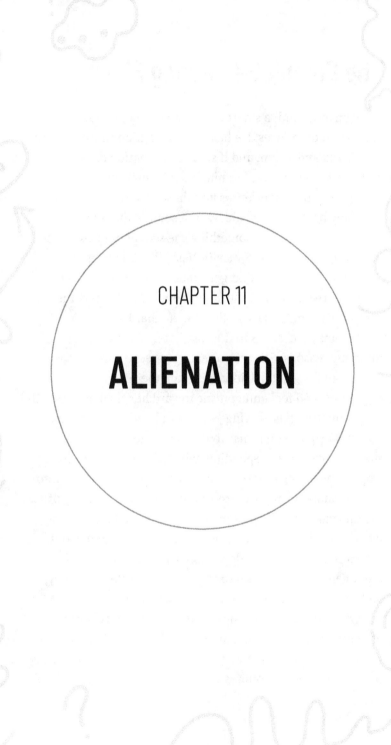

CHAPTER 11

ALIENATION

The Completely Wrong Place

Early on as a child, a smart teen begins to hear about other places and other lives. He hears about fashion shows in Paris, New York, and Milan, and if some combination of factors make fashion important to him, then he may already be pining for those experiences and those places even though he may only be eight years old. Or if it's music that moves her deeply, then it may be something she sees about Nashville or Austin—a reality show set in Nashville, an old episode of *Austin City Limits*—that gets under her skin and makes her think two things: "I must get there!" and "I am in the completely wrong place to live the life that I want to live."

She may feel she is in the completely wrong place for many reasons. She may already possess a subtle understanding that patriotism is often the refuge of scoundrels and feel antagonistic toward her small town's self-congratulatory flag-waving. She may already comprehend how unfairly wealth is distributed and hate her family's status, privilege, and spending habits. She may have already stopped believing that the religious group she was born into has a monopoly on goodness or any real understanding of the universe, and she may even have come to hate the prayer meetings in her parents' living room. As we chatted about earlier in the section on deception, by virtue of her native intelligence, she is bound to see through a lot of hypocrisy, and that will make her want to be elsewhere.

Of course, she can't know that "elsewhere" is hardly all that her heart is telling her it's cracked up to be. All she knows is that she is in a very wrong place, among very wrong people, encircled by oppressive beliefs and naked prejudices that don't suit her, and maybe caught in the wrong time as well. Idealizing Paris in the 1920s or Greenwich Village in the 1940s, she may pine for a different epoch, perhaps one where she could write with a quill pen. This time, as well as this place, may not suit her.

However, she is where she is. Unless her life is so dark and turbulent and she is so distraught or unsafe that she runs away, taking to the dangerous life of the streets, she is functionally trapped. Her only real escape is her room. A smart teen will spend a lot of time in her room not just because it is private and cozy, but because it is her sanctuary, where she can believe what she believes and be who she is.

If what I'm describing is true for her, she will feel alienated from the world in which she is forced to live. Her most pressing thought may be, "I have to get out of here," and her plans may revolve around escape. This sense of alienation and of a pressing need to get away can lead to all sorts of impulsive escapades, from pregnancies ("Motherhood will get me out of here!") to world-crossing escapes ("I must spend the summer with my Irish cousins!") to the ever-increasing consumption of drugs ("If my body can't be elsewhere, my head can!") This kind of alienation is all too likely to create both angst and dramatic, life-altering consequences.

For Parents

You may not recognize the extent to which your smart teen is feeling alienated; or you may recognize it but not understand it. Remember, however, that you chose your life: she didn't choose hers. She didn't choose to live, say, in a small town with its small-town prejudices, or to attend an expensive, fancy school, with its competitive, off-putting classmates. Given her druthers, she might well have chosen Paris, or public school. Acknowledging her rather complete lack of decision-making power may help you better understand her feelings of alienation.

And you may be feeling the same way. You, too, may be feeling alienated. Many smart adults are. You may not be feeling very much at home in your skin, your house, or your town. If this is how you're experiencing life, wouldn't it be lovely to sit your teen down and share that news? Maybe by saying something like "Isn't it weird here?" Maybe you could laugh together or cry together. Maybe you could start reading absurdist literature together and start your own two-person discussion group. Consider: Is it possible that sharing would serve both of you?

We have arrived at a time in human history where every young person is exposed to a million possible worlds, many of which will not speak to her but some of which will speak to her powerfully. Naturally, she will want to be in that world, not in her everyday world. This desire alienates her from her day-to-day life and causes a pain that is hard to address. Help her by understanding that it is no criticism of you if she is dreaming about and perhaps even obsessing over other universes. And if it is a criticism, well, let that be her right. She is entitled to feel as if she is in the completely wrong place, since she didn't choose this one.

For Teens

You may feel that you are in the completely wrong place. And you may be. But, for now at least, you are where you are. It is in your best interests to figure out how to live exactly where you are, without creating unnecessary emotional anguish and without driving yourself to the edge of a cliff, beyond which are those many potentially dangerous escapades.

Let's think about that. How can you best manage to be okay exactly where you are? What might a plan for that look like? This isn't the "getting away" plan—the escape plan—but the "what's the best way for me to cope while I'm here?" plan. There are some simple things you might try, like putting up posters of where you want to be. Let's start there. What are some simple things that you might try to help you live well exactly where you are, trapped in a world not of your own making? Try your hand at generating that list.

The Nocturnal Liberal Queer Atheist

Countless studies have tried to get at what, apart from raw intelligence, distinguishes smart folks from other folks.

For example, studies seem to show that intelligent teens are more likely to be left-wing liberal, atheistic, queer, and nocturnal than the general teen population. (See, for example, "Intelligence and Homosexuality" by Satoshi Kanazawa in the *Journal of Biosocial Science*.) Kanazawa presents some interesting hypotheses from evolutionary psychology as to why this might be the case. But of course, no one knows for sure. Still, these are darned interesting findings.

We can certainly recognize this person. We can see him or her in our mind's eye at some late-night poetry slam or at some all-night diner, writing her screenplay. And we see that she is also watching her back. This person—this nocturnal liberal queer atheist—is not society's darling. She certainly has a society in which to fit, from gay bars to folk cafés to college support groups, and a culture to partake of and participate in. But out in the world, she had better be careful. Aren't secrecy and danger major parts of the basic coloration of her life?

We are just half a century into homosexuality not being treated as a mental disorder by the American Psychiatric Association, the self-proclaimed arbiter of mental disorders. Likewise, it has only been half a century since homosexuality was decriminalized in many Western countries. In some places, it's hardly been two decades. In a whole host of places, it hasn't happened yet. As of this writing, sixty-nine countries still have laws on the books criminalizing homosexuality.

So what is it going to be like for a nocturnal, liberal, queer, atheistic teen in Afghanistan, Ethiopia, Algeria, Jamaica, or Uzbekistan? Hell, probably. Or in a small town in Texas or Mississippi? Hell, probably. Or in any red community or any red family? Hell, probably. In addition to everything else coming at her hormonally, interpersonally, intellectually, and identity-wise, here is this elephant in the room: that she is despised by a sizable portion of the world's population.

This reality amplifies our understanding of why a smart teen might crave some stop on the International Bohemian Highway, some Greenwich Village or Left Bank, some Los Angeles or Berlin, where she can feel safe and where she can be herself. In that Greenwich Village women's bar or that Parisian jazz club, she can look for love, raise her voice, and feel her power. There, she is not an alien. There, she can almost relax. No wonder getting there is on her mind!

Many smart teens do not fit this liberal, atheistic, queer, nocturnal profile. But many do. If you are the parent of one, what is your number one priority? To love them. Your first priority is not to feel guilty, angry, or disappointed, but to love them. Your nocturnal liberal queer atheist teen is exactly who they are. Let them know that you see them.

For Parents

It goes without saying that your smart teen may not be like you. But she may be *very much* not like you. She may come from her own planet and inhabit her own world. If you take that as an affront, or if you take that as a tragedy, then you have built a wall between the two of you. Your teen, too, will likely erect a wall to protect herself from scrutiny and reproaches. She will keep her secrets hidden behind that wall; she may keep much of her life hidden behind that wall. Given that there may be a stone wall between the two of you, what do you want to do? To ask the question differently: How will you go about loving your child with a wall between you?

For Teens

If you are this nocturnal liberal queer atheistic teen, how you decide to live will depend a great deal on how your parents and your siblings react to you. If they accept you, you can have one sort of life. If they can't accept you, you will be forced to live another sort of life. If this is all mixed up, with your mother accepting you, your father appalled by you, your younger sister allied with you, and your younger brother more appalled than your father, you will necessarily have to walk on eggshells, thankful for the support you have but nevertheless trapped in a hostile environment.

What should you do? Three things: First, feel good about yourself. You are not a misfit, sinner, or weirdo. You are not damaged goods or some horror movie mutation. You are exactly the young person you are, smart, compassionate, left of center, gay, the enemy of hypocrisy—in short, quite an excellent piece of work. Others may want you to feel bad about yourself. Do not buy their vision. They are looking at the world through the small eyes of hatred. Number one: Feel good about yourself.

Number two, be safe. The world is a dangerous place. Bullies and haters have existed since the beginning of time and will be with us as long as we are around as a species. Be yourself—but be careful. If you are living in a cosmopolitan, left-leaning pocket of decency, that is one thing. But if you are living in one of the world's many ordinary yet inhospitable and unsafe places, be very careful. Adopt as your mantra, "I am taking good care." You may feel a deep desire to be reckless and unsafe so as to throw off your yoke of oppression and to thumb your nose in their faces, but try to let that desire quietly dissipate. Number two, let your mantra be: "I am taking good care."

Number three, absolutely, deeply, and completely believe that your future will be better than your present. Maybe you are currently miserable. Maybe you feel trapped. Maybe you can't see anything ever fundamentally changing, not in your family or in the world, nor in life. Shake yourself out of the belief that the future must be as dark as the present. It need not be. Your life in a big city or in some bohemian town, with your future loving partner, doing rich, meaningful work, is coming. It can be coming…if you don't give up now. Number three: Intentionally cultivate the awareness that it gets better.

Search and Rescue

Children grow up believing in quests: in the quest to rescue the trapped princess, the quest to return the magic stone to its rightful place, the quest to save the world from fire-breathing dragons. All this fantasizing about quests has the insidious effect of buttressing the powerful, unfortunate, and ubiquitous two-thousand-year-old metaphor that we are to search for meaning, that the search for meaning is also some sort of quest, that meaning has been lost or stolen, that it is out there somewhere, and that we had better go find it or else stand bereft of meaning.

This conglomeration of Disney fantasy, hero's journey mythology, and fundamental misunderstandings about meaning seeps into a smart teen's pores and alienates him from everyday meaning-making, from the meaning that he could be experiencing when he plays catch with his younger brother, laughs at his great-aunt's stories, or says a few words to that cute girl in algebra class. He could be experiencing meaning in countless ways each and every day of the month, if only he didn't have it in his head that meaning was "something very different from this" and "somewhere very far from here."

Everything he does and experiences stands in relation to this myth and comes out second best. Play catch with my brother when there is a guru in India who knows so much? I must meet that guru! Enjoy my great-aunt's stories when they have nothing to with the history of philosophy? I should be consuming medieval philosophy! Flirt a little when God has some mysterious plans for me? Back to the bible! In such ways the here and now can come to feel completely inferior to some idealized, mistaken vision of a faraway world where "real meaning" is experienced.

It would be lovely if children were taught that there is nothing out there and that there is nothing for which to search, and as a result were rescued from the alienating mythology that the here and now is inferior to something labeled "spiritual," something that is ticking away on a clock they can't see and can't fathom. Their teen years could become prime meaning-making years if they were helped to discern what is important to them and if they engaged with those important things. The result would be the experience of meaning.

Not only would they experience much less alienation, they would also learn a most amazing skill: how to coax meaning into existence by turning their thoughts and feelings about what is important into life purposes. They could stop jumping into the empty sea, hoping to find a sea creature or a secret and often only drowning there instead, and learn how to translate the values and principles they want to uphold into a way of life that suits them.

Instead of feeling that they ought to be searching for meaning because it seems to be lost, they could stand tall, experiencing themselves as existentially solid. What lesson could possibly benefit them more?

For Parents

It is quite likely that your smart teen is wounded in a way that you can't see, wounded in the area of meaning. This is not located in a physical place on her body and there is no doctor to consult, certainly not self-proclaimed soul doctors. The wound is caused by her misunderstanding of the nature of meaning, a misunderstanding that you may share. You, too, may feel that you have never found what you were looking for, that you never arrived at that port where meaning was docked. If you do feel this way, read on, as what I have to say to your smart teen may amount to important news for you as well.

For Teens

If you are feeling alienated from the present moment and from your present life, a large part of that alienation may be coming from this idea you have, promoted and supported by a variety of master narratives, from God narratives to quest narratives, that there is something "out there" from which you are currently separated. That felt separation is terribly painful and may make you desperate to "find it," leading you to some occult church or some far-flung expedition.

The truth, which you may not be able to hear at this moment and which may take you a lifetime to really process, is that the meaning you crave is just a certain sort of subjective psychological experience, something more like a feeling than anything else, something that comes and goes inside of you, just as joy comes and goes and anger comes and goes. It is not something that is "out there" for you to find. Once you process this truth, you can make your way without those painful feelings of separation and alienation, living your life purposes, whatever you decide they ought to be, and making your way in life.

Life can feel meaningful right now if you can let go of the idea that there is more to life than life. There is no extra-life something to hunt, as if everything hinged on finding a particular white elephant. If you can let go of that idea, you can begin the long process of feeling through what's really important to you, whether that's love, physics, political action, adventure, family, ancient history, nature walks, building with your hands, abstract math, or all of the above in your own amazingly idiosyncratic mix. Not a one of these is more "spiritual" than the other, "spiritual" being a trap word used to suggest that meaning only exists in certain places "out there," in places like hidden lakes that take days to find, or guru-led communities, or vaulted cathedrals.

You are the arbiter of what you consider important. If you focus on what you yourself believe is important in life, life will feel meaningful to you some of the time (but not always, because meaning, like any feeling, is bound to come and go). Heal the wound caused by the mental mistake that you are separated from something—from gods, from arcane knowledge, from robed figures, from universal secrets— by letting go of the idea that you are separated. There is nothing to search for in the realm of meaning. When you stop searching because you have seen through that myth, you will find yourself rescued from alienation.

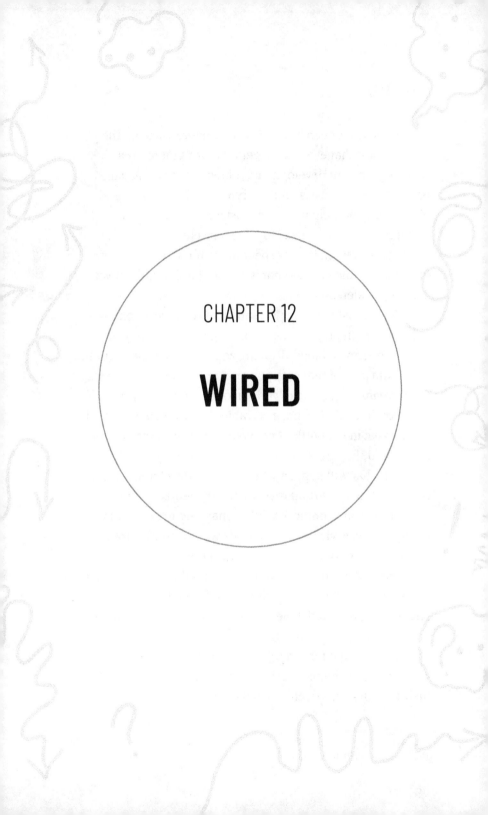

CHAPTER 12

WIRED

Online

There has never been anything even remotely like it. The online world that every teenager takes for granted is a shockingly recent development, allowing teens in Japan, Brazil, Sweden, Russia, and everywhere else to transcend place and to participate in the most amazing warren of rabbit holes ever created. How are teens reacting to this amazing development? By spending a full nine hours every day online. Nine hours—that is at once hard to fathom yet perfectly understandable.

Why not listen to that Korean band with its billion followers, then play a super-realistic game in which you defeat an army of blood-dripping zombies, then check out the Instagram post of that cute guy or cute gal half a world away, then stream an episode of your favorite series? Why not? Why not, indeed? It is inconceivable that this genie can ever be put back in the bottle. And would we even want to even if we could?

And what will happen when the next development really takes hold, when virtual reality and augmented reality are ubiquitous opportunities? What teenager won't be virtually killing zombies, virtually having sex with beautiful strangers, virtually being somewhere else, anywhere else, anywhere but in his airless room, surrounded by his dirty clothes? I am no futurist, but the handwriting is on the wall. Cyberspace, screen time, that dark hole where light can't escape—more of that must surely be coming.

No small chapter can say much about this sea change, where one day, human beings may spend just about all of their time in front of screens and on devices. Maybe that day is already just about here. And with it will come more of all of those strange maladies of the twenty-first century: cyberbullying, old men posing as young girls, blatant and clever efforts to steal your identity, opportunities to create a billion-dollar business with an idea you penned on a napkin, and that new mania, the mania of the next and next and next and next.

How does this affect a smart teen? First, she will be no less susceptible to these blandishments than the next person. It is just too attractive, too compelling, too just about necessary. Second, she will remain absorbed, as every teen is now absorbed, when she is on one of her devices; but the second she leaves her device, she will likely find herself horribly antsy and unable to concentrate on anything. We see this "full absorption followed by hyperactivity" all the time nowadays. If online is the new drug, hyperactivity is the new withdrawal symptom.

The brain is an odd device. It allows you to sit for hours on end, completely absorbed in the post-apocalyptic creature you are cartooning into existence. But it does not allow you to take in even one word of what your history teacher is explaining about the Thirty Years War. The brain of a smart teen can stay absorbed for enormous amounts of time online, fiddling with his music-making computer program; but it then provides him with the attention span of a gnat when, no longer absorbed, his brain darts from here to there to nowhere, with his body following, depositing him first on the sofa, then on the floor, then bouncing him off the walls.

What metaphor to employ? Online time as drug? Online stimuli as obsession? Online virtual environments as vicarious living? Online as hothouse and playground and hiding place? We thought that television had grabbed the human mind by the throat and would hold it hostage forever. Then, ready or not, came cyberspace. Who can avoid—or even minimize—its hypnotic vise grip?

I asked my Russian granddaughter Katya to share her thoughts on how the online world is affecting her and her friends. She explains:

> Teenagers use the Internet to express themselves, share their feelings, thoughts, and ideas, and create supportive community. We find it a very important place and a great opportunity. But it also comes with a significant dark side. It can be too easily used to make up for what we're missing in real life, and using the Internet that way is both exhausting and pretty unsuccessful. And there are lots of other problems, too.
>
> Because being on the Internet is so convenient and doesn't come with the same consequences as real life, it's easy to avoid real life. We can miss out on learning how the real world operates and miss out on the opportunity to meet new, interesting people. Instead of meeting real people, we can spend countless hours on Internet relationships where we never meet the person we've gotten close to.
>
> We might share everything with that person, including political and philosophical ideas, and do this for ten years—and never see each other, never meet each other, and never want to meet each other. It's like we don't want reality to intrude on the

relationship and we don't want to be disappointed by who our dear Internet friend is in real life.

Then there's the problem of role playing. The person you think you're in a relationship with may only be playing a role, and you yourself may get sucked into playing some sort of role. You might do this to entertain yourself, and the other person may also be only trying to entertain himself. I know people who never reveal their names and it's all a game for them, they may even play a role that is exactly the opposite of who they really are.

For others, it is no game at all, it is very serious. One of my friends is having a distant relationship, he and his girlfriend are in touch all the time and they have serious plans for the future. For them, it is hard to make others understand that it's not a game, but a real relationship that they intend to keep building. We are supposed to do everything we can to protect what we love, so if we have a serious relationship in the digital sphere and our parents say that it's going to lead to nothing, we are not going to want to hear that—and we won't.

On the Internet, we face many of the same problems we face in real life. We can feel like we have to be perfect and feel bad if we say or do something that feels less than perfect. If a teen puts out some creative work on the Internet, well, criticism there will hurt just as much as does criticism in the real world. For me, when I publish a photo of myself and see "likes," my self-esteem automatically rises. When I don't publish anything, I feel like people have forgotten about me or even that they don't like me anymore.

Consciously, I know better; I know my own value, and I know that my friends and the people who love me don't forget about me. I know that my relationships with them don't hinge on whether I've posted a photo or shared something live. But still it's hard not to get caught up caring about how you look and how you're perceived—and hard not to spend every day on the Internet. It's an addictive process, searching for ego satisfaction and gratification in cyberspace.

It can be hard to remember that what happens in the digital world isn't the way things will happen in life. The digital world lets us use our imagination and lets us live in a fantasy world, which is very attractive to creative and smart teens. For us, it is especially hard not to become addicted because we are getting to create our reality, which is something we love doing—except that it isn't reality. But we can convince ourselves that it is and stay in cyberspace far too long.

One answer is to do a digital detox. In the Jewish culture, and based on religious principles, Shabbat is a day of the week when no electronic devices are allowed, and I can see the sense in that. Everybody could try to dedicate one day of the week, not necessarily Saturday, to family life and to life offline. My generation is used to spending a good portion of every single day on the Internet, pretty much living on social media and in cyberspace. It's hard to see that changing much—but taking one day a week off might help.

For Parents

How attached are you to your own devices? Probably very. Your smart teen, having teethed on cyberspace, is even more attached. It may be more natural for her to text than to talk and to surf than to think. That old-fashioned experience of sitting in a sunny corner reading a good book in a silence so complete that the drone of a single fly buzzing sounded like a Halo helicopter is not dead, but it is definitely on life support. We can just about kiss real silence goodbye.

You can't unplug your smart teen from her devices, but you can create cyber-free moments by taking a phone-free walk with her, a mania-free, destination-free, even conversation-free oasis of actual air and actual sun and actual movement. This is bound to do the two of you some good in all sorts of ways, not the least of which may be that you will be providing an opportunity for your smart teen to say something, perhaps something that has been on her mind but that has remained unspoken. There is no "answer" to cyberspace; but mustn't a good half-hour or hour of unplugging still be possible?

For Teens

It will go in one ear and out the other for me to say limit your screen time, be judicious about how you operate online, be smart about how your own appetites and desires get hooked by all that easy availability—for shopping, for sexualized escapades, for glancing friendships—and take stock of what your online immersion is doing to the rest of your life. How could that sentence not go in one ear and out the other?

But you may be quite aware that when you try to concentrate on something that requires a certain sort of silence and a certain sort of patience, you can't. You get fidgety and your mind wanders—likely to a device. You need your phone, you need to check something, you need to text someone, you need to do something out there somewhere, rather than remaining in your own mind, where the real work gets done. If you are aware of this dynamic and you are not too happy about it, you might think about creating a program for retrieving your brain from cyberspace. Wouldn't it be lovely to get your brain back?

Attention/Deficit

It is very common for a client of mine to believe that he has an "attention deficit disorder" and *that* is what is preventing him from penning his novel or getting his journal article written. Although he may not have been officially diagnosed, he is convinced that he has it, and that it is because of his disorder that he can't concentrate, can't get his work done, and can't get things completed. And his next question is to ask, shouldn't he be on medication?

Does he have a disorder? Or is it rather that a combination of low-level anxiety, the speediness of the online world coupled with the speediness of the real world, a racing brain, a million worries and distractions, and an indwelling style that supports a lack of concentration all are conspiring to produce the things called "attention deficits," leading to the popular label "attention deficit disorder"?

To my mind, it is the latter. And if it is the latter, then chemicals are not the answer.

To label something an "attention deficit disorder" begs the question of why should it be easy to pay attention? You are trying to write a history paper for school. Nothing about it interests you. You try to pay attention, but it is physically painful to write yet another paragraph on the legacy of Spanish priests in California. For one thing, you doubt that any of what you've read is truthful. For another, this Spanish priest looks indistinguishable from the last one. For a third, you could be enjoyably killing zombies and moving from level six to level seven of the game you're playing with zombie killers worldwide. Who could possibly pay attention?

The experts claim that paying attention should be a snap and that not paying attention is a mental disorder. But doesn't it feel truer that a lack of attention is rather to be expected? That doesn't make it any less of a challenge, but it does relocate it back into the territory of the normal. These lapses of attention, possibly caused by ambient anxiety, a racing brain, boredom, an "I can't concentrate" self-identification, or maybe caused in some other way, are both natural and predictable. But of course, that doesn't make them any less challenging, not if you are trying to get that history paper written—or trying to do anything that requires concentration and intellectual stamina.

For Parents

You may have felt for the longest time that your smart teen wasn't doing a very good job at paying attention. This may have been a problem all through his school years, from kindergarten on, and years ago, you may have started down the road of mental disorder labeling and chemical strategies. This may be a significant issue of long standing for you, your smart teen, and your whole family.

Maybe this is a moment for you and your smart teen to revisit the whole attention question. If it is, and if he is willing, you might support him in putting into place the five "attention helpful" strategies I've listed below. You and your smart teen might put your heads together and ponder what environmental changes might help and what family dynamic changes might help. You might do a little research and locate an anxiety management podcast, a mindfulness video, or an online relaxation program to pass along. This might be the perfect moment to start fresh in your thinking about what "a lack of attention" might signify—and to come up with some completely new approaches in collaboration with your smart teen.

For Teens

If you have trouble concentrating, rather than bad-mouthing yourself or labeling yourself as having a disorder, try the following five gambits.

First, learn an anxiety management technique or two. Anxiety is likely the culprit. Learn a breathing technique, a mindfulness technique, a relaxation technique. This is number one.

Second, decide not to flee because something is boring or because some shiny object has caught your attention. Say, "I can stay put," and mean it. Yes, you may be bored. Yes, that shiny object is winking at you. Yes, you may feel anxious. Accept the reality of these distractions and pressures, and return to your mantra: "I can stay put."

Third, try not to catastrophize, overdramatize, or in other ways think thoughts that undermine your native ability to concentrate. If you're thinking, "This is too hard!" or "I've never been good at this!" or "I don't understand this!" or "I hate this!"—each thought coming with a dramatic exclamation point—you are undermining your ability to concentrate. When you hear yourself thinking one of those thoughts, say "No!" to it.

Fourth, be safe. If we don't feel safe, it is hard to concentrate. If it doesn't feel safe at home because that's the scene of past traumas or because home life is chaotic, work in the school library or your local library. Your environment matters. If it's noisy, raucous, or unsafe at home, of course you'll find it hard to concentrate there.

Fifth, consider how useful the ability to focus on what is before you will be in multiple ways in your adult life. Get a clear picture of how calmness and an ability to concentrate are going to serve you as you try to live your life purposes. Connect up "paying attention" and "having the life you want." They do connect!

Help yourself pay better attention by employing these strategies. If you refuse to try these strategies out, honestly accept that you have refused and that you are less interested in paying attention than you claim to be. That would be important news worth thinking about.

Productive Obsessions

In this section, I want to present you with the ideas that there are two kinds of obsessions, productive ones and unproductive ones, and that while the second are terrible, the first are rather wonderful. Unproductive obsessions rob of us intellectual power, squander our time and our energy, and hijack our brain. Productive obsessions, by contrast, are the way that our brain dives into something worth thinking deeply about. You do not want unproductive obsessions. You do want productive obsessions. There is a world of difference between them.

Rather than thinking about a million things, which amounts to thinking about nothing, and maintaining only a low-level interest in and enthusiasm about life, a smart teen might announce to her brain that she has a fine use for it and that she intends to move it to a higher gear. It is an engine meant to perform in that higher gear; and since her brain was only waiting for her invitation, it might just respond beautifully.

Most of our obsessions are not of our own choosing and do not serve us. They are unproductive and harmful. They arise because we are anxious creatures and our unproductive thoughts cycle repeatedly, pulsing to the beat of that anxiety. Against our will, we unproductively obsess about what a friend said, catching a dreaded disease, or failing our next test. We unproductively obsess about things that we hope will happen, like being chosen for the English prize, and about things that we don't want to have happen, like getting pimples. Our mind, which ought to be ours, is stolen away by anxiety thieves.

The money-focused culture applauds this brain abdication; it needs you to care about the latest movie, the latest gadget, the latest sermon, the latest investment opportunity. Every aspect of the culture has something to sell you and is looking to grab your attention. Marketers do not want you to be thinking too deeply about your budding symphony or your scientific research and miss their sales pitch. What if you didn't check your email every few minutes? What good would their banner ads do? Your productive obsessions—your brainstorms—are dollars out of their pockets.

For Parents

Unproductive obsessions, and the compulsive behaviors associated with them, do not serve us. They waste our precious time and occupy our finite neurons, robbing us of their availability, and they pressure us to behave compulsively in ways that amount to further self-disservice. Anxiety fuels these obsessions, and our efforts to relieve our anxiety often leads us to pointless, questionable, or dangerous behaviors intended to quiet our nerves and banish the anxiety.

Our own nervous system puts us under enormous pressure and produces all sorts of unhappy effects in addition to our unproductive obsessing. We become hypervigilant, easily startled, prone to opportunistic illnesses, unable to sleep, and easily fatigued. Anxiety throws us a party of problems, with unproductive obsessions the guest of honor. You do not want this for yourself, and you do not want this for your teen.

But think about the distinction I am making between unproductive obsessions and productive ones. How could anything great or large be dreamed into existence without someone thinking long and hard about it? You might have a profitable conversation with your teen about this distinction. Just bat it around and see what the two of you think. It might make for one of your more valuable and interesting chats. And, who knows, the chat might serve you just as much as it serves your smart teen.

For Teens

People waste their brains. They allow themselves to worry about next to nothing, wasting neurons; they allow themselves to grow numb with distractions, wasting neurons. Because they have not trained themselves to aim their brain in the direction of rich and rewarding ideas, ideas worth the wholesale enlistment of neurons, they stay mired in the brain equivalent of a rat race, with the brain spending its neuronal capital on spinning hamster wheels.

Try not to let this happen to you.

Productive obsessions, by contrast, are wonderful. Scientific obsessions lead to vaccines. Artistic obsessions lead to symphonies. Humanitarian obsessions lead to freedom and justice. Productive obsessions are our lifeblood, both for the individual and for all of humanity. We should not fear them simply because they put us under unwonted pressure, give a compulsive edge to our behaviors, or in other ways discomfort us and threaten us. Rather, we should learn how to encourage them and manage them.

It is up to you whether you will dumb yourself down or smarten yourself up. If you opt to smarten yourself up by cultivating rich ideas that have weight and worth, you will get to make meaning in ways that few people experience. The person next to you may think that the epitome of powering up one's brain is a sharp game of bridge or a rousing fight with a crossword puzzle. I hope you agree that real brain power is the holding of a rich idea over time as you productively obsess your novel into existence, build your remarkable business, or aid in the understanding of some profound scientific puzzle. These productive obsessions may be coming!

You can learn to opt for brainstorms you choose and for big thinking over time, and by doing that, you will fulfill your promise—and your promises to yourself. An idea for a novel sparks your imagination, or an idea for an Internet business wakes you up in the middle of the night, or a problem in science grips you; in each case, if you allow it to take up your attention, it turns into a potentially productive brainstorm. A brainstorm is the full activation of your neuronal forces in support of an idea that you intend to cherish and to elaborate, so powerful an activation that it amounts to a productive obsession.

Unproductive obsessions, no way. Productive obsessions, yes! Take a little time and consider this distinction.

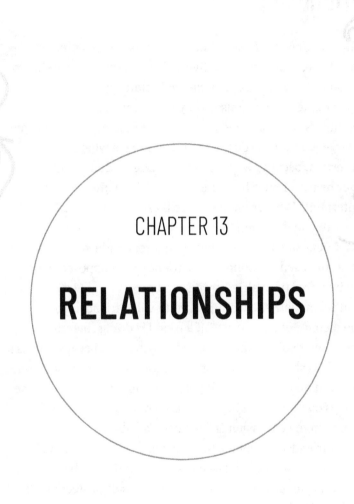

CHAPTER 13

RELATIONSHIPS

Friendship

There is a genre of reality television show with a premise that goes as follows. An individual or a couple are looking for a home. They are asked by the real estate agent what they are looking for in a house. They pretty much always reply, "Stainless steel appliances, two sinks in the master bathroom, a large yard for the dog, and an open space where we can entertain, because we love entertaining!" I don't think I've ever heard a house hunter exclaim, "Oh, by the way, I hate to entertain!" What friendly people these shows attract!

Are you that friendly?

Friendships are complicated matters. Indeed, what is the idea supposed to connote? Are friendships supposed to be entirely free of rivalries, status, and power struggles? Does that seem real? Are we supposed to value friendship over the dictates of conscience? If a friend is doing something unconscionable, is she supposed to get a pass because she is a friend? Is she still a friend if she becomes busy with someone else and maybe enjoys that person's company more than she enjoys ours? Has she betrayed us by having friends she likes more? In the end, what is friendship all about?

Is friendship about actual trust or about mere shared interests? Is it a little bit—or a lot—sexual? Is it about gathering allies and forming a clique for self-protection? Is it about holding sway over another person or about another person holding sway over you? Is it about acquiring a drinking buddy or a cigarette buddy? Human beings like to keep things simple—too simple—and bandy about a word like "friendship" as if its meaning was transparent. It is anything but.

Like everyone else, a smart teen is stuck wanting friends because of what friendships can provide. She may also be stuck with finding friendships burdensome when they suck time and energy and just aren't serving, stuck not being sure if she even likes, respects, or values her friends, and sometimes stuck with being overinvested in a given friend because life would feel just too cold and lonely without that friend.

Melanie, a coaching client, explained:

> In high school, I made friends with anyone who was verbally quick. So, our friendships really revolved around being ironic, sarcastic, and caustic. This was the so-to-speak ideal way to get through high school, except that in retrospect, it was actually a pretty cold and cruel way of being. I can't say that I liked my friends much, or the "me" I was when I was with them. On the other hand, they probably were exactly the right friends for me because together, we warded off the stupidest aspects of high school. As the saying goes, it was complicated.

And friendships can be wonderful. A single friend can make the difference between an unbearable year and a bearable one, or between a bleak high school experience and a tolerable high school experience. Friends can be allies, protectors, supporters, witnesses, and more. We want and need friends, since they provide camaraderie and human warmth. We just have to be careful and look at each relationship squarely to make sure that it brings more positives than negatives into our lives.

For Parents

You are entirely entitled to have opinions about your smart teen's friends. If you smell danger, trust your nose. If something seems off, if your teen is being put down, if your teen has stopped studying, if your teen is especially secretive, if your teen is dressing as provocatively as her new friend, or even if you can't quite put your finger on what's disturbing you, speak up. You are entitled and obliged to speak up about what you see.

Then, listen. Give your teen time and space to answer. Her first reaction will almost certainly be stubborn defensiveness. But that doesn't mean that she hasn't heard you and that she isn't thinking about what you've said. Explain your worries, give her a chance to think, invite her to walk and chat, and be available in case she is willing to communicate. The seemingly innocent stroll through the park that ensues might prove a game-changer, a life-changing moment. Life is like that.

For Teens

Friendship is an area of life where it is easy not to be smart. You might follow a friend down a foolhardy path for the sake of friendship. You might cover for a friend for the sake of friendship. You might take abuse from a friend, ignoring the abuse for the sake of friendship. That you are smart doesn't make you the least bit immune to the way that the word "friendship" can hold you hostage to an unsuitable or unsatisfactory relationship.

Do not expect your friendships to be straightforward or easy. They are complicated, dynamic relationships entered into for all sorts of reasons. Take your time before fully recognizing an acquaintance as a friend. An acquaintance need not be elevated to the lofty status of friend until you've tested the waters. Even once preliminarily approved, he or she is still in a kind of probationary status. The painter Georgia O'Keeffe once said, "To have a friend takes time." It does take time, because we are monitoring the relationship to make sure that it serves us and that it makes sense.

You want friends who are friends. Real friends are about the best thing in the world. But you also want to be savvy about who you consider a friend and whether or not you lift an acquaintance to the lofty status of friend too quickly. Be real about how the person behaves. Be real about whether or not his values match yours. Be real about whether or not you trust him or even like him. And if it's the real deal, then be a good friend yourself. That may take work on your part, which may stretch you, but genuine friendships are worth it.

Sex

Sex is a game-changer for all human beings and especially for teens. What teenager isn't thinking about sex a lot of time? Freud may have lavished too much attention on sex as *the* driving force in human affairs, but he was certainly not wrong to put it at the center of the picture. It is a pleasure, yes, but it is also a disruptor, a distractor, and even a game-changer. And it is that even when—let us pay homage here to two of Freud's defense mechanisms—it is being repressed or sublimated.

Freud argued that human beings often did X in order to avoid thinking about and doing Y, when Y was dangerous or unavailable and when X was socially sanctioned and aligned with the individual's values. How does this apply to a smart teen? Well, how many smart teens are getting good grades because they aren't having sex? And what may happen when, as can occur, they do start having sex? There may go the grades!

How many smart teens have started getting Cs in their junior or senior year because they are embroiled in their first tempestuous, sexy affair? Who can possibly think about any chemistry besides interpersonal chemistry when the sex starts?

Apart from all the obvious dangers of teenage sex, from unwanted pregnancies to sexually transmitted diseases, and from interpersonal dramas and personal crashes, there is the central, basic, almost-never-named crisis that can occur when one moves from sexually dormant to sexually awakened. That awakening often isn't like a flower opening but more like a pressure cooker blowing its lid right off.

Then there is the other side of the coin: wanting sex but either not getting it or avoiding it. Many smart teens will get through their teenage years as sublimating virgins, because the urge hasn't quite arisen in them yet, because they are suppressing the urge, because they are too shy, awkward, aloof and "out of it" to be a player, or because they don't know how to play the game. If they are not yet in the game, it may do wonders for their grades—but what is it doing to their psyche?

What, then, do we have? We have one smart teenager in a loud turmoil over actual sex and another smart teenager in a quiet turmoil over no sex. Is there some wonderful middle ground where a smart teenager has lovely, brilliant, safe, psychologically uneventful sex with a charming partner, with no crises around pregnancies, jealousies, misunderstandings, marriage proposals, boredom or anything, while continuing to pay perfect attention to her grades and her extracurricular activities? How often does life paint that picture? Has it happened even once?

There is no answer to the question of sex. For a smart teenager, one with a vivid imagination, high hopes, and keen sensitivities, sex may hit him or her like a ton of bricks. It may change the color of life from one day to the next from an orderly thing, as orderly as lining up one's toys or books, to a disorderly thing, as disorderly as awkward physical interactions in the backs of cars. Through carefulness or defensiveness, this day may get pushed into the future, past the teen years and into young adulthood, but once it comes...well, try to reason with a hormone. Can even massive intelligence do that?

For Parents

I do not need to tell a parent of a teen that sex may become an issue. There is nothing much that can help with that or make sex go away. But you can notice what you notice and say what you need to say. You can say that you are there for your teen; that you are on your teen's side; that you have been there yourself; and that you are not going to be able to stop yourself from staying up late, worrying, harping, and all the rest, because you know about life's dangers.

Have as your message, "I'm going to listen to you, I trust you, but I am going to say what I need to say to you." Then, like every parent since the beginning of time, cross your fingers. Be observant, be direct, and be kind; sex is walloping your teen just as it walloped you.

For Teens

Picture the room that is your mind. Picture yourself sitting in there on your easy chair, looking at the wall opposite. What do you see there? The sign in bright green neon that you yourself have hung there. What does that sign say? "Make good choices."

Will you? Ah, well, not always. You can take that to the bank. Against your better judgment, you may fall for someone who is mean just because he or she is attractive. You may do something in the moment that you instantaneously know was a mistake. You may get so darkly jealous that you find yourself hiding in the bushes, shaking your head at your own antics. You may fight with your parents, even though you know that they are only worried about you. Are these among your "good choices"? No—and you know it.

But keep that phrase in mind and don't abandon it even if you slip and make some terrible choices. Believe in your heart that you have it in you to make good choices and that those good choices can and will add up to a good life. One bad choice may have real consequences, but it doesn't predict a lifetime of bad choices.

Nature created sex to be an insistent sort of thing. It provided orgasms as a payoff but decided not to prepare us for the dramas, crises, and pain that come with sexual reality. So, we are unprepared. If that first love affair produces amazing pain, know that you are in good company. This is what human beings experience. That you have the top grades in French or are good at calculus is not going to make a whit of difference when it comes to nature's blockbuster, sex.

Peers

Nowadays we use the phrase "peer pressure" to stand for a teen's spiderweb of peer interactions. But much more goes on than the phrase "peer pressure" can capture. The world of peers is where experimentation happens, where what you wear and how you look matter, where gossip and sexually transmitted diseases circulate, where bullying is a fact of life, where one measures oneself, tests oneself, and feels the piercing gaze of a thousand eyes. Nothing about peer relationships is straightforward. For some smart teens, there is also nothing about them to recommend them. Martin, a coaching client, explains:

> When I looked around, I couldn't find a single place to fit in. These were kids my own age who had grown up in the same city and in the same era as me, watching the same things, listening to the same music, and yet they could have been from another planet as far as I was concerned. I understood their words but not why they were saying them. I

understood their interests but not why those things interested them. All day long I was shaking my head internally, going, "Who are these kids?" and "What's wrong with me?" I experienced no peer pressure because these kids weren't my peers, they were aliens from outer space.

John, a coaching client, had a very different experience. John explains:

> I was smart, but I was also good at baseball. That allowed me to fit in and not get tagged with any egghead labels. I played the role of jock; I was a natural third baseman—good reflexes, a good arm, an instinct for guarding the line—and I was good in the clutch. So, I was pretty much a hero type. The super-huge downside was the whole jock, paramilitary, initiation, cruelty-called-pranks side of team sports. It is extreme to say it, but you could read fascism in the way the coach coached and in the way that players responded. Finally, I rebelled, and that was the end of my "good" high school experience. I went into books and suddenly I had no friends, just about from one day to the next.

Nowadays, a peer may be someone in chemistry class, but also may be someone five thousand miles away with whom a smart teen is flirting. And that faraway "peer" may be a forty-four-year-old man in disguise. No teen can completely avoid this peer tornado, even if he wishes that he could, because he must pass among his peers and interact with them daily. That is his world, like it or not.

For Parents

Given the difficulty of making sense of our own relationships, what are you to make of your smart teen's relationships, most of which are not visible to you? You don't see them, you don't hear about them; that whole secret world goes on completely out of view. Yes, you may get a glimpse of your smart teen's world at the track meet where she's competing or at the band concert where she's playing. But that will only be a hint. All the rest would require an archaeological dig.

And your smart teen won't let you dig there. But you can inquire. What might your opening salvo be? Certainly not, "How's school?" But maybe some out-of-left-field inquiry like, "Anyone bullying you at school?" or, "Have you found a nice clique?" or, "What's the difference between a pier and a peer?" (Possible answer: One you walk on, and the other walks on you.) Of course, you wouldn't expect your smart teen to stop everything and really answer. But who knows, maybe later that evening she will want to chat. That would be lovely, wouldn't it?

For Teens

You may be a smart teen who has a lot of dynamic interactions with your peers. Perhaps this is because you want those interactions, because you're trying to get along, or because those interactions are forced upon you. Or you may be a smart teen who keeps himself separate from his peers and hardly notices their existence.

In the first instance, you'll have to deal with the competitive energy, the gossip, the petty cruelties, the romantic entanglements and the rivalries of that busy, closed society. In the second instance, you may find your sense of isolation, alienation, and loneliness exacerbated by your having distanced yourself from your peers.

Because of your powerful need to maintain your individuality, because of your natural ability to see through falsehoods, and because of the other qualities that combine to make you an outsider and a rebel, if you repress all that and try to fit in, you may fit in only at the cost of emotional distress; yet if you act on your individual impulses, the chances are slim that you will be able to fit in or that you will want to do so.

Is there some possible middle ground? There might be. It might be that you can keep the full universe of your peers at a distance but still have an excellent time with some subset of that universe, like the drama club, chess club, math club, French club, or the band. That subset could perhaps be your world and those teens your self-selected peers. That has a chance of working!

Peer pressure matters. This is a place to be smart. Your brain knows how to calculate the consequences of actions. What is the downside of hanging with the druggies? What is the downside of using your body to make friends? What is the downside of choosing the popular kids, if they are cruel and take pleasure in humiliation? You are smart enough to see which way is up. Use the freedom that you know you cherish to free yourself from peer relationships that are bankrupt or that harm you.

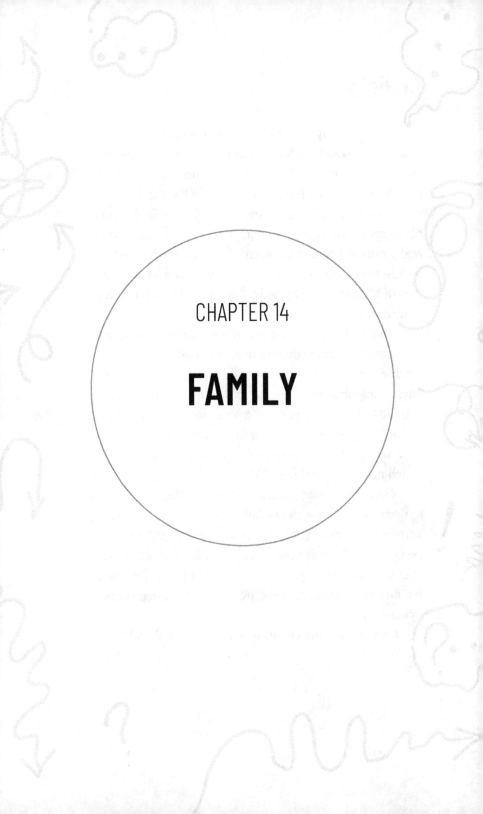

CHAPTER 14

FAMILY

Collisions

When I was young, I thought I might become a physicist. I especially liked the idea of particle accelerators. Believe it or not, our math-and-science high school had one in the basement. Students built it at a cost of $10,000. (By contrast, the Large Hadron Collider cost $6.4 billion to build and took thirty years to complete.) I don't think our cyclotron ever really ran—if I remember correctly, when it was fired up, it tanked the electrical system in the building and in a whole part of Manhattan's East Side. But, well, it was the thought that counted.

What went on in a particle accelerator seemed to me like some charming combination of a chariot race, a pinball machine, and bumper cars. And so I thought, "Why not? Physics might be fun." Lots of collisions! But collisions in real life—well, that's another matter entirely. And collisions in the family are especially no fun. Much of family life is experienced that way, not as interactions but as collisions—which makes family life prickly.

A smart teen may collide with her mother about what to wear, or collide with her father about his political beliefs. Perhaps she collides with her brother about just about everything. There are collisions over curfews; collisions over spending money; collisions over dating; collisions over screen time—opinions colliding, values colliding, sparks flying everywhere.

Joan, a coaching client, remembered her prickly family life:

My father was a tyrant. He was very smart, which made him think…I don't know what, that he had the right to look down on everyone. Just passing by him felt dangerous. Not that he was physically assaultive, but it always felt like he might be—he felt like a living threat. So we all avoided him; except that he was also like a magnet, as if his threatening nature provoked us to tangle with him, maybe to prove that we weren't cowards.

I fought with him endlessly over whatever position he took on anything. If he was for a Palestinian state, I was against it. If he considered veganism idiotic, I became a vegan (for a while at least). If he said that 2 + 2 = 4, I would come back with, "Not in higher mathematics!" We never just talked. We always butted heads, like two rams locked in a pen.

The special collisions that a smart teen can expect are verbal ones, since she is smart and her parents may well be smart also. The whole family may be good at arguing and at picking apart arguments. This verbal sparring is not only corrosive but sets in motion a lifelong dynamic, one where smart kids become smart adults who are adept at using words to fight—and to harm. This "skill" will prove useful if a smart teen becomes a trial lawyer—but in the rest of life, not so much.

A smart teen who is passive, on the other hand, may not do the colliding herself but may end up doing a lot of ducking. Wearing her headphones to muffle the tumult and hiding out in her room to avoid becoming collateral damage, she is nevertheless painfully affected by the hubbub. She may find it hard to concentrate on her homework, leading to poor grades; she may feel physically ill, leading to lost school days, or feel chronically anxious, leading to binge eating or secret pill popping, or grow to despair of the situation, leading to inertia. If where you live is under siege, it is not just the combatants who are affected. Even babies can feel the tension.

For Parents

Everyone has a part in family collisions. What is your part? That's the first line of inquiry, to figure out your contribution to family squabbles, verbal spats, and tense confrontations.

If your mate seems to be the prime instigator, then you have a responsibility to say something to him or her for the sake of your children. And you will have to say it more than once. You may need to say it every time he or she blows up, creates some unnecessary drama, or behaves meanly. Of course, this will not prove easy. Of course, this will not feel safe. Of course, this will amount to a collision of its own. But you know it's necessary, don't you?

It may be that everyone in the house has a share of the blame. But that is the opposite of saying that therefore no one is to blame. Five wrongs do not make a right—they only make for harm and chaos.

For Teens

The best policy with regard to family collisions is to get out of the way, if that's possible. In some households, that isn't possible. Your parents may intrude so forcefully or battle so loudly that your room is not your sanctuary. If you can't get out of the way at home, then spend extra time in your school library or a town library, at a friend's home, or in a congenial café where you can get your schoolwork done, where you can think, and where you can feel safe.

Think, too, about your part in these family collisions. Has it become your habit to do battle about nothing in particular just to preserve your sense that you are not giving in? Are you experiencing standing your ground over small matters as worth it or as serving you? And are you possibly instigating some of these collisions? How is that working for you?

Family collisions are emotionally painful and psychologically damaging. You can't control others, or even influence them much, but you can be thoughtful about your part in these collisions—and thoughtful about what you can do to stay out of their way.

Adverse Childhood Experiences

Could there be a drier label for horrible things happening than "adverse childhood experiences"? But that is the phrase we currently use to capture experiences including physical abuse and verbal abuse, emotional neglect and physical neglect, domestic violence, and parental separation. My own primary research is in the area of adverse childhood experiences I've named *authoritarian wounding*, that is, the harm done by an authoritarian father, mother, or sibling. Millions of smart teens have suffered in these ways in the past, and others are suffering right now.

Does a smart teen react to these events differently than other teens? Quite possibly. We can guess that any or all of the following might occur. Given his vivid imagination, he may lose himself in fantasy, creating harrowing graphic novels that he keeps to himself. He might experience his existential anxiety, which is already pronounced as he worries about life's meaning and purpose, significantly increasing as he tries to make sense of these questions against a backdrop of cruelty. He might well see his naturally large appetites, which come with high intelligence, transforming into addictions, and so on.

One main result is that he is likely to become less smart. Let me share a very technical paragraph from a journal article, and then let's chat about it a bit. Here is a portion of the abstract from an article entitled "Evidence That the Impact of Childhood Trauma on IQ Is Substantial in Controls, Moderate in Siblings, and Absent in Patients with Psychotic Disorder" (in the *Schizophrenia Bulletin*, March 2017, at https://pubmed.ncbi.nlm.nih.gov/28177077/):

"Research suggests that childhood trauma is associated with cognitive alterations, but it is not known whether the cognitive alterations observed in patients with psychotic disorder, and their relatives, is trauma related. Patients with a schizophrenia-spectrum diagnosis (n = 1119), siblings of patients (n = 1059) and healthy comparison subjects (HCS; n = 586) were interviewed three times over a period of six years. Repeated measures of IQ were analyzed as a function of childhood trauma and group, controlling for confounders. There were significant differences in the impact of childhood trauma on IQ across the three groups. Exposure in [healthy comparison subjects] was associated with a nearly five-point reduction in IQ (-4.85; 95% confidence interval [CI]: -7.98

to -1.73, P = .002), a lesser reduction in siblings (-2.58; 95% CI: -4.69 to -0.46, P = .017) and no significant reduction in patients (-0.84; 95% CI: -2.78 to 1.10, P = .398)."

The very idea of IQ tests is old-fashioned, and highly controversial to boot, and IQ scores may mean nothing to a contemporary parent or his or her teen. But these so-to-speak findings are nevertheless suggestive. They suggest that for a child with a so-called mental illness, trauma does not particularly alter his intelligence (and it would be interesting to discuss why that might be the case). But in so-called healthy children, *trauma produced nearly a 5 percent reduction in IQ scores.* Skipping over the questions of what IQ tests actually measure or whether the construct is valid or relevant, this is nevertheless an eye-opening finding.

To follow this logic, a child with a "natural" IQ of 140 will slowly end up with an IQ nearer to 130 by virtue of exposure to childhood trauma. Can that be felt by the child? How might that be experienced? Would it be a distraught shaking of his head as he can't answer questions that he knows that he should be able to answer? Or would it present as avoiding mental tasks because he feels "too stupid" to tackle them, even as he knows "somewhere inside" that he was built to handle them? What would the experience of losing IQ points to trauma feel like, and what would the consequences of that loss amount to?

We are just scratching the surface here. The relationship between trauma and intelligence is unexplored territory. But important relationships must exist. You are smart—and then harm happens. Surely that is going to affect you. And might not that harm even be life-altering?

For Parents

Let me not presume that you are the problem. But what if your mate is? What if you are partnered with a cruel, bullying, punitive partner who lays down strict, arbitrary rules, intrudes where he shouldn't, belittles your teen, and makes everyone's life miserable? Is the problem then your teen's poor grades or your mate's authoritarian personality? What do you think?

This section is about adverse childhood experiences, which means that you may well be implicated in the problem. It is hard to say that and quite likely hard for you to hear that. But you are reading this book, so part of you is a truth-teller. If the trauma your teen is experiencing is ongoing, please help to stop it. If it is in the past but still a pressing part of her life, as emotional pain, school troubles, relationship difficulties, diminished intellectual abilities, or in some other ways, be as honest as you can in making the connection between your teen's current troubles and what has gone on before in their experiences.

For Teens

If you've suffered from adverse childhood experiences or other traumas and difficulties, the result may be that you are currently less smart than you otherwise would have been. Is that potential smartness recoverable? We do not know and probably can't know. But we can act as if it is. We can hold out the possibility that healing would produce a smarter you. Let us hold out that possibility!

How might that healing happen? By getting psychological and physical distance from any current abusive relationship, if that is possible, by cultivating advocates and allies, by engaging in peer counseling or other forms of support, and by learning about "trauma-informed self-care." Engaging in these efforts will serve not only your emotional life but your intellectual life as well. Your suffering may likely have hurt your intelligence, and your healing will likely improve your intelligence. When you think about it, isn't that sort of amazing? To maybe get back ten IQ points that you didn't even know were stolen from you?

The Life and Death of Imagination

A smart child is curious. That sounds like a blessing and a benefit, but it often isn't much of one in real life.

Most human interactions are conservative by nature. A religious father or mother doesn't want a curious child asking impertinent questions. Imagine little Bobby asking his religious parents, "How does God pick the four hundred people He kills in a plane crash?" Or, "Why does God care if we use one set of plates for dairy and another set for meat?" Such questions will anger most religious parents. Their child will get that she has angered her parents and then will have to decide whether being curious is worth the family drama.

Their curiosity is inconvenient at best and quite likely antagonizing. So after a while, a smart child will settle into one or another of the following relationships to his own questioning nature:

- He may still ask questions, but he may come to expect a nonresponse or a hostile response, which produces an oddly caustic parent-child dynamic.
- He may still ask them, and if as a result, he is then labeled a wise guy or a smart aleck, it may become clear to him that his very presence irritates his family, and he may start to self-identify as an irritant, an outsider, or even an outcast.
- Wanting to get along and desiring parental approval, he may stop asking questions, leading him down the path of conventionality, where such questions are closeted and tabled, or even a strategy of suppressed creativity. As Elaine, a client of mine, put it, "My strategy as a teen was to stay under the radar and avoid conflict. I never promoted myself, I never asked questions, I never took center stage. Although I knew I was intelligent and creative, I was submerged by fear of criticism and abhorred exposure. And so, I didn't imagine and I didn't create. This was not laziness; it was fear and a lack of clarity about how to proceed despite my fear."

Even in progressive households, and sometimes especially in progressive households, a war goes on between supporting a child's creative imaginings on the one hand and demanding good grades and an unblemished academic path on the other. It is charming that the four-year-old brings home a highly imaginative drawing from preschool. But by the teen years, when her parents are thinking about "the best colleges," competition for scarce resources, and "making it" in life, then her taking time off from getting good grades for the sake of some blue-sky imagining is much less permissible. A summer camp devoted to theater improvisation? Poetry slams rather than history homework? Please!

A smart child wants to know. But that curiosity is bound to produce all sorts of consequences, which may range from self-imposed silence to a sarcasm that translates as, "Boy, am I surrounded by hypocrites." Then high school arrives, and with it, more of the same. A smart teen's curiosity will be channeled down acceptable paths, like the school's chess club or math club, damned by teachers with faint praise ("That's a very interesting approach, Mary, but not the assignment at all"), or outright squelched. She will deeply and completely come to comprehend the extent to which her curiosity is not welcome at home, at school, or anywhere really.

As her imagination dims, something dark happens. The death of imagination in a growing child can cause life to lose its grandeur, its spark, and its meaning. If you are living a constrained life but also can't imagine some shining city on a hill, some stop on the international bohemian highway, or some amusing story that keeps your spirits up, that constrained life shrinks even smaller. Imagination breaks constraint; and if that imagination flickers out, it's as if the windows of your mindroom have been painted black.

For Parents

Now that your teen is a teen, her charming drawings from preschool are far in your rearview mirror. Now you want her to succeed, not imagine. You want her to draw within the lines, not erase the lines and redraw them to her liking. You know why you want this, and it no doubt seems sensible to want this. But it would be good if you could appreciate the cost of a forced lack of imagination. Can you support your teen's blue-sky reveries and her flights of imagination, even as you strive to keep her within the lines? That is a good conversation to have with yourself.

For Teens

You may have arrived at a place of fear and suppression, not wanting to be seen, not wanting to provoke your teachers or your parents, not wanting to do anything or say anything that is going to make you feel unsafe or bring down the roof on your head. But if you've at least retained a life of the imagination, you can dream, plan, fantasize, and keep your spirits up using your brain's ability to build fortified castles and imagine great escapes.

Try to protect your imagination. You may have to learn facts for the chemistry test, but between bouts of studying, imagine a universe where a million hydrogen atoms bond with one oxygen atom, creating something wild, funny, and lifesaving. Nothing—not texting, not posting a picture of your cat or your mocha, not gaming, not grabbing a cigarette, not turning up the music—is a substitute for going inside and imagining. Don't let the forces of family, school, friends, or society shut down your curiosity, your connection to truth, beauty, and goodness, or your powers of imagination.

A person's imagination can vanish, leaving him dull, brittle, conventional, and unimaginative. He may well feel this loss without being able to name it and wonder why he can't write his novel, compose his concerto, or dream up elegant math solutions. Can he pinpoint that his imagination got stolen somewhere along the line? Probably not. Please watch out for that theft as you traverse your teen years! If that theft happens, that won't be a petty theft but a grand larceny.

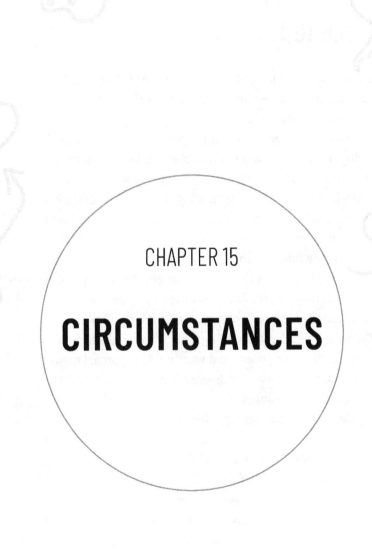

CHAPTER 15

CIRCUMSTANCES

Inhibited

Each smart teen is located in a particular sea of circumstances. She may swim there; or she may discover that she is drowning there.

One smart teen grows up in poverty and finds herself living out of a car with her out-of-work dad. Another grows up in a cult. A third must contend with famous parents. One has a high-achieving older sibling, another a disabled brother who requires what seems like the family's whole attention. One smart teen can travel to Europe, another must work to support the family. Circumstances matter.

One of the ways that circumstances matter is the way in which they can inhibit a smart teen and prevent her from manifesting her potential. It is hard to think if you are in danger, if you are hungry, or if the adults around you are slamming doors and warring. Many smart teens find that their native intelligence is held hostage to their difficult circumstances.

Maryanne, a coaching client, explains:

There was a lot in my childhood that I'm thankful for. I had plenty of opportunities to read books, build dens, climb trees, draw, and learn a musical instrument. There was magic and wonder. However, my parents also struggled with marital issues, with money worries, and with their own mental health challenges, as well as caring for my disabled brother. I was a sensitive kid, and my antenna was highly attuned to the stress around me, so I escaped into my imagination a lot.

I knew from the age of six that I was supposed to be a writer, and I also knew that I loved art, music, and performing. But I just couldn't get on with any of that. The slightest criticism from a teacher stopped me dead in my tracks. I couldn't concentrate. I spent time in my mind, but not productively, not in a way that supported real effort or real creativity.

Something in me shut down creatively because of all that stress, and when it did, I no longer had any way of processing that stress. I was an anxious kid, and by the time I became a teenager, I was internalizing everything; I became even more anxious, socially isolated, and dislocated. It was like I couldn't find my center or settle into my body. I had this phantom self who was a writer, but I couldn't get her to come and live in me full time— or even a little. This has continued into adulthood.

It is odd how little a teenager's circumstances play into how the mental health establishment views her distress. It is a thousand times easier for a psychiatrist to run down a checklist and pronounce a teen clinically depressed than to attempt to fathom the gestalt of her life. This checklist approach takes minutes and leads to an easy answer— chemicals—while teasing out what is actually bringing this girl to her knees might take who knows how long. The idea that circumstances don't count is built into the current mental disorder paradigm, for obvious reasons. It is ever so much easier to prescribe than to inquire.

Circumstances matter. Nor can a smart teen do much to change her circumstances, short of running away, a desperate act that is unlikely to turn out very well—and one that will inevitably drop her in yet another set of difficult, or worse than difficult, circumstances. An adult can divorce, leave her job, move across the country, start a business, stay with a dear friend, train for a new life, and create a new life. A smart teen can do none of these things, which means that she must deal both with her circumstances and with the pain and stress her circumstances may be causing.

For Parents

Here is an area where you can possibly really help your smart teen. Her circumstances are largely in your hands. If you and your husband are screaming at one another, you could stop screaming. That won't have solved your marital problems, but it would surely help your smart teen concentrate better. If it is long past time for your smart teen to stop sharing her room with her younger sister, finally clean out the spare room and give them both room to breathe. These are things that you can do.

There are almost certainly things for you to try that would improve her circumstances. Identify them. Better yet, identify them together. Pull out two pads and two pens and invite your smart teen to join you in improving her circumstances. Suggest that each of you create a list, then compare notes. Your lists may align or may look completely different—they may include far too many items about which neither of you can do a thing, or they may be full of cross-outs and second thoughts. But you will have made a start. Could you possibly spend a more profitable half-hour together?

For Teens

It would be a mistake to suppose that your circumstances don't matter, that you are somehow supposed to be so strong, resilient, and bulletproof that you can just soldier along, impervious to what is going on around you. No, what is going on around you really, really affects you.

If you think that some particular change might be possible if only you alerted someone that you need that change, please speak up. If there are improvements that you yourself can make, please make them. These may amount to no more than a drop in the bucket—or they may do a world of good. You can't know until you try.

To repeat the headlines of this section: Circumstances really matter; most of the circumstances of your life will not be in your control; this will produce stress and other serious consequences; so, try your hand at two things, changing what can be changed and adopting some stress management strategies. Here is an area where you can employ your smarts. What can you possibly do about your circumstances? Bravely challenge your neurons to ponder that question.

Inside/Outside

People have different experiences of life. In any given small town, I might be a member of the lone Jewish family, the lone Syrian family, or the lone Chinese family, and I am likely to be very aware that I am an unaccepted and only reluctantly tolerated member of this small community. This may not play itself out on any particular day, but I likely know not to display a menorah in my window at Christmas time, or wear a hijab, or try to celebrate Chinese New Year too publicly.

Words like class, race, prejudice, bias, and bigotry represent real things in the real world. A smart teenager, in addition to feeling alienated for all the reasons we've discussed, is also a member of a majority culture or a minority culture and may feel alienated in either camp. If he is part of a majority cultural group, he is likely to feel alienation because he sees clearly how privilege operates and doesn't want any part of it; and of course such feelings may also come up for a member of a marginalized cultural group.

On the one hand, this is simple to understand: You are either inside or you are outside. But the subtleties of inside and outside are quite phenomenal. Is a light-skinned African American woman more outside or inside? Might she be scorned by her peers for looking too much like the ruling class? Are a secular Jew and an orthodox Jew sitting together on a park bench in it together as members of the same group, or are they completely separated and alienated from each other?

If you are the parent of a smart teen, you may have reconciled yourself to all this long ago, having decided to hide out as a member of a minority, having decided that no one, inside or outside, can really be trusted, or having decided to play along with the "whole Christmas thing" at your Christian in-laws. Likely, you have found your way, whether or not it sits comfortably. But your smart teen is nowhere near finding his way. This is an in-your-face issue for him as he tries to figure out how to choose his friends, which groups to join, and even just how to be when he's invited for a meal at his Japanese, African American, or Muslim girlfriend's home.

For Parents

You are either inside or outside, and you are bound to communicate to your children exactly what that means. You will teach them how to keep their head down and when to hush up, if you are outside, and how to speak to maids and how much to tip bellhops, if you are inside. All of this you will communicate. But do not be surprised if your smart child or your smart teen comes back with "Why?" and "No." They can't possibly understand all the ramifications of class, race, religion, nationality, ethnicity, and human divisiveness, but they have a keen sense of fairness and may simply balk.

You may, in fact, know best. You may understand real world dangers much better than your child does. You may understand the value of group solidarity in a troubled world, even if you don't love all of your group's values or practices and even with the understanding that an "us" versus "them" mentality keeps the world troubled. And if you believe that you are right, how can you allow your child to make what you deem are terrible decisions? Isn't this one of those horrible parental dilemmas, one with no good answers?

What you can do is communicate to your smart teen that group divisions are a blight as well as an incontrovertible reality, that he is bound to make his own choices but that you are obliged to point out what you feel is true, and that you will listen to what he has to say and hope that he can listen to what you offer. Whether you are inside or outside or have found a place on the sidelines, you have seen the troubles, and your experience is something you can communicate.

For Teens

Because you are smart, you understand that we are one species and that the divisions separating human beings are essentially terrible. But they exist, and they can only be ignored at your own peril. These divisions—and with them, ill feelings, assaults, civil wars, atrocities, and all the rest—are not going away in my lifetime or in your lifetime. It may not be at all clear to you where you belong, who can be trusted, or what constitutes "inside" and "outside," but what should be indubitably clear to you already is that these bitter divisions matter.

They matter to you in a special way, because as a smart teen, you understand that it makes no sense to align yourself with the "inside" or "outside" just because you were born there. You may not agree with the values and principles of your group, and you may see no reason to support those values or abide by them. But by taking that sort of stand, if you take it, you will be angering "your people" and distancing yourself from them. I think you can see how you might end up precarious and alone, intellectually secure but socially bereft.

There is nothing like an answer to this dilemma. If you are outside, that will cost you. If you are inside, that may also cost you, as you find yourself dutifully aligning with a group that you may or may not like or respect, causing pain to your conscience; or as you righteously rebel, costing you privileges and opportunities. The only part-answer is to tread warily, understanding that this species of ours is not very compassionate, not very flexible, and not very forgiving.

Shifting Landscapes

The following happens all the time: A child is creative. He draws well, tells interesting stories, and loves to act. This charms his parents. They provide enrichment activities like art classes or acting camps. Without giving it much thought, they presume that their child's creative urges are a kind of sideline, off to the side of what their child will really do in life. Of course, he will become a lawyer or a doctor and not a cartoonist. How outlandish, that he might become a cartoonist! Then, one day, often in their smart teen's junior year of high school, as he engages with the college application process, they suddenly learn that he means to be an art major, an English major, or an acting major. Then all hell breaks loose.

For both parent and child, life can look one way today and a very different way tomorrow. One day I was a freewheeling eighteen-year-old who had just flunked out of college and was spending my time hitchhiking around the country. Then suddenly, I enlisted and became a soldier. For one smart teen, the changed landscape may have to do with deciding from one day to the next to skip college and volunteer in Africa. For another smart teen, it might be the decision to leave his comfy home with his dad and help his down-and-out mom by getting a job in a big box store.

Landscapes can shift dramatically, in life-changing ways, often for no other reason than a thought percolating up—*I think I'll enlist, I think I'll volunteer in Africa, I think I'll help my mom out*—and turning "just like that" into a rock-hard plan that no one can dispute.

One face of this shifting landscape dynamic is the way that the pesky question "What do you want to be when you grow up?" is always in the back of a smart teen's mind. He may not be consciously turning this question over as he muddles through gym class, but it is always there somewhere, acting like a kind of lens through which life is viewed. He passes by the scene of a blazing inferno: "Would I like to be a firefighter?" He goes to the courthouse to apply for a passport: "Would I like to be a judge?" He may not know that any of this daydreaming is going on somewhere inside of him, but it is.

It would be odd if a tribal youth living a thousand years ago was asked that question, "What do you want to be when you grow up?" A contemporary smart teen is pestered by that question precisely because he or she can "be anything." She can build apps or fly jets or trade stocks or open a café or train to be a clown. She can study the history of the world's religions, the nature of cell structures, or how to build bridges across wide rivers. And her choice will be…

All of this musing and confusion is going on somewhere inside a smart teen's psyche. Out of this roiling may come what looks like a snap decision. One moment, life looked this way—now, who can even recognize it?

For Parents

On a given day, you and your family may seem to be on something like solid ground; yet the very next day, here comes the earthquake. You wouldn't think that life could change on a dime—that it could change so quickly as to allow zero time for a single breath and so radically as to be just about unrecognizable. But it can, and it often does.

The particular shifting landscape we're focusing on is the one where your smart teen drops some bombshell like, "Oh, by the way, I intend to study cartooning in college" or "Oh, by the way, I'm skipping college and volunteering in Africa" or "Oh, by the way, I'm dropping out of high school to get a job and help pay my way" or "Oh, by the way, Jessica and I are getting married."

When this bombshell is dropped on you, try not to reflexively go to war and dismiss your smart teen's decision out of hand as preposterous or ridiculous. But you are not obliged to smile and accept it. Your response might be, "That's a lot to take in," followed by, "Can we chat about this tonight at seven?" Give yourself time to think and space to breathe. Then, when you reconvene, you might ask, "What's going through your mind?" Let him speak. Listen. Nod, meaning that you are hearing him, not that you are necessarily agreeing. Then you might say, "Okay, let me think about all this," and set up another meeting. This will give you a chance to muster your arguments and stop reeling a little.

For Teens

We are chatting not about circumstances changing but about your inner landscape changing, and life-altering consequences that will follow. One minute, you were obviously going to college. Then, through some unconscious process, you made the decision to postpone college and volunteer in Africa. That's the sort of shifting landscape we're examining.

Your new decision may feel set in stone and quite incontrovertible. I would nevertheless ask that you get a second opinion from yourself. The question to ask yourself isn't "Is this the right decision?" (because it will feel as if it is) or "Where did this notion come from?" (because, well, who can say?) Rather, the question to ask yourself is, "Can I tolerate holding this as an open question and not a settled matter while I give this some more thought?" I hope that you can. The whole rest of your life may hinge on this decision. Surely you can spare a little time and space for your own second opinion?

Giving yourself that time and space may prove amazingly difficult, because the moment we make a decision of this sort, we often become stubborn and refuse to look at it twice. We do this in part because we don't want anyone, ourselves included, to talk us out of our decision. Try not to go to that stubborn place. Rather, stand there, look at your new plan, and be a little amazed at how things have shifted inside of you from one moment to the next. Try to peacefully ponder your choices, giving each one its due. College or Africa? There's a lot to think about, isn't there?

CHAPTER 16

SCHOOL

Five Ordeals

Compulsory education is a year-in, year-out reality for much of the world's children. Hardly any child experiences school as an unmitigated joy, and many experience it as an ordeal. Why an ordeal? Let's take a glancing look at five of these ordeals: exams, school spirit, boredom, homework, and romances.

Formal education comes with testing. It might be a rope-climbing test in gym class, an essay test in English class, a vocabulary quiz in Spanish class, a final project in shop class, or a state-mandated multiple-choice test meant to gauge your grade level. The tests just keep coming. Most smart teens will feel obliged to treat them as if they matter because they want good grades so that they can go on to a good college. And when something matters, that raises their anxiety level. A test for a C student may mean nothing more than "another C coming," not causing him enough stress to even raise an eyebrow. But a test for someone who needs all As is an event on his anxiety calendar.

Then there's school spirit. The same fervor that makes for football riots, as the supporters of rival teams clash "just because" (which also can engender wars), creates a school atmosphere that a smart teen is likely to hate, one that she may try to avoid at all costs. These pumped-up rivalries between her school and other schools are unlikely to strike her as innocent fun because even without studying history, she knows where pitting one group against another group leads. She may go to the Friday night basketball game because everyone does, and she may even get caught up in the moment and cheer, but when she hears the team's star guard explaining that God helped them to victory, she will cringe. She knows that school spirit is a form of jingoistic posturing and at root a kind of hatred. For her, pep rallies may well fall into the "ordeal" category.

Then there's the ordeal of boredom. Most classes are boring. We are not built for hour upon hour of boredom, but we learn to cope, letting our mind wander, doodling, half-listening and half-dozing, secretly working on our novel, or as one famous actor put it when describing how bored he was in school, by "drinking ink." A smart teen is likely to be especially bored, perhaps even excruciatingly bored, as her math teacher goes over elementary material for the tenth time for the sake of the students who haven't grasped that material yet. Isn't something mischievous, impulsive, and maybe even dangerous brewing during all those hours of boredom? Boredom is both an ordeal and a danger, as a bored mind almost can't help but dream up some misadventure.

Homework is a fourth ordeal. School does not end at 3 p.m. A teen is obliged to write papers, study for exams, work on joint projects, and all the rest, with each subject's teacher piling on more homework, oblivious to what that accumulated pile might look or feel like. This would matter less if one could just blow it all off and do the minimum, as any C student just waiting to turn sixteen and get the heck out of there might do. But no, a smart teen is obliged to take these assignments seriously because she wants and needs the grades. She must contain her trickster impulse to write a sarcastic paper for English and is required to write a serious one instead. She must do what she knows she has to do to get her A and then deal with her headache.

A fifth ordeal is so combustible as to be explosive. That's the hothouse ordeal of sexual attraction, sexual fantasies, and school romances. From day to day, it is the experience of the shifting of sentiments and alliances: You like her, but she likes him, so you hate her; but she says a nice thing to you and now you love her once more—but she's suddenly ignoring you again. Being smart provides absolutely no immunity against this hormonal chaos. (I served in Korea, which has about as many landmines as any place on earth after high school.)

For Parents

It is fine to say to your teen as she leaves for school, "Have a nice day!" But be aware of what her days feel like to her. Just as your days at work are anything but easy, with quotas to meet, complaints to handle, bottom line concerns to address, and all the rest—causing an estimated 75 percent of all workers to hate their jobs—your smart teen's days at school are likely anything but easy. And then comes homework.

If you can, share a laugh. You are each facing your secret ordeals, all of those things that you don't want to talk about with each other. But see if you can share a show, a laugh, a bowl of popcorn—something. See if you can carve out a no-ordeal hour for the two of you. That might make more of a positive difference than you can possibly imagine, for both of you.

For Teens

Tests, crushes, team spirit, boredom, homework—what a life! Even as these and the many other ordeals we've discussed come at you, keep returning to your belief in yourself, your commitment to making good choices, your wisdom that "this too shall pass," and your vision of a bright future where you get to think, create, love, and live a life of purpose. The danger is that these ordeals will wear you down and make you sick, emotionally and physically. Be as careful as you can be and let these pressures wash away with each hot shower you take. See if you can turn "ordeal" into "no big deal." If you can, that will be splendid!

Talent as Demand

Once a smart teen gets it into his head that he is good at something, that "something" often becomes a kind of demand, something insistent, something that he is "supposed" to pursue. That knowledge may come at a very young age, as soon as school starts or even earlier, as he sees that he can do math faster than other kids, that he is quicker at chess than all of his little friends (and most of the adults he plays), that he is a better storyteller (the one who puts red herrings into his mysteries so as to make them more interesting), or the first one to come up with answers in every subject, because his brain is firing on all cylinders.

With the knowledge that he has certain talents comes pressure. Where will this pressure come from? From inside—

from the child himself, and quite possibly from one of his or her parents as well. To take one example, we recently watched as a "stage mother" literally pushed her distraught-looking daughter the entire length of the walkway leading to the stage—a good hundred feet of pushing, all the way to her solo dance performance. That was pressure not as metaphor but as a relentless push in the back.

This demand is highly resistant to reality testing. Few teens with, for instance, a talent and love for acting will countenance the thought, "Only a handful of actors make it out of the tens of thousands who try." They know this to be the truth, but they can't allow themselves to acknowledge this truth. Their love frequently drops a veil over it, and this "ambition plus love" equation has them applying to colleges with the best theater departments.

If it turns out to be more ambition than love, how difficult those next years will be! There you might be, a performance and composition major, adding thousands of hours to your cello practice, composing pieces for classes that do not genuinely interest you, wearing yourself out in the service of "the cellist's life" while becoming clearer and clearer that you are good, but not one of the world's top cellists, and never allowing yourself a thought which might break your heart but also liberate you: "Shouldn't I be doing something else?"

It is wonderful that you can do something well. But try to avoid the trap that comes with talent. That you can do something well doesn't mean that you must do that thing. Your talent may serve you beautifully, but it should not be worn like handcuffs. What makes for a good life is that you are living your life purposes, not that you are blindly serving a talent. Hopefully you will make use of your talents in the service of your life purposes–but that would be you making use of them, rather than you being held hostage by them.

For Parents

You are bound to discover that your relationship to your teen's talents is a complicated one. On the one hand, why wouldn't you take pride in the fact that he is good at something? Why wouldn't you support him at getting more proficient at that something by paying for lessons, camps, classes, workshops, and whatever else might serve that talent? At the same time, you can see a shadow darkening the picture: how the talent is taking over; how fierce competition is filtering its way into the equation; how life seems to be narrowing to include that talent and little else; and how internal pressure to excel is producing anxiety and draining joy. The talent may be wonderful, but it is no unmitigated blessing, is it?

You may be one of the lucky parents for whom this all works out beautifully as your teen's talent for and love of biology translate into a brilliant research career or a happy life as a pediatrician. But do count yourself among the lucky ones if that happens. For many parents, the picture will look much murkier. Should you support the talent while cautioning against overinvesting emotionally in it? Or should you join with your teen in his dream and do everything in your power to help him achieve his dream, even as you secretly doubt his chances and doubt even whether he is really in love with it or just trapped by talent? How will you play this?

For Teens

Just because you can run fast doesn't mean that you must train for the Olympics. Talent doesn't have to come with some built-in demand attached. Even if you are talented at something and love it, like playing the drums, playing chess, sketching, or solving math problems, that doesn't mean that you *must* become a drummer, chess player, visual artist, or mathematician. You may want to and that may be the right choice for you, but that is different from *must*.

It is good to be real. You may be very good at chess, but will you ever progress past one thousandth in the world? Let's say that you make it to number nineteen or number nine. Will those thousands of hours of playing chess have served you? Let's go all the way and make you world champion. Do you want to be world chess champion, or to have lived a very different life from that one? You get to answer that question any way you like; but it would be good if you pondered it before putting in all those thousands of hours.

Talent is wonderful and talent is demanding. Try to free yourself from its demands. If you can do that, you will have better positioned yourself to make use of your talents in the service of your truest intentions.

College

Do smart teens experience college as a joyful place of growth and meaning? Or do they experience it as something darker and different?

We expect a smart teen to head right off to college, maybe with a gap for a bit of exploration and travel but with not too long of a gap. College is supposed to come next, directly after high school. And what if you have no idea what college is for, if no subject particularly interests you, if your "dark night of the soul" is consuming you, and you really need something other than college? No matter. College is meant to come next and almost certainly will come next.

This makes nineteen one of the most potentially dangerous years of your life. And the statistics bear this out. The freshman year of college is a tremendously difficult year for teens. For many, there is weight gain associated with plentiful dorm food, social eating, and the freedom to eat too much, leading to a typical fifteen-pound weight gain in freshman year. There are the powerful stressors of dorm life, difficult or boring classes, forced closeness, and distance from family and friends. And for a smart teen especially, there is the darkness, nowadays labeled "depression," that comes with going through the motions in what may feel like an alien and alienating environment.

This darkness is largely a product of the following: You are nineteen, full of life, maybe boiling over with desires, and at the same time, you find yourself demoralized by the reality of college life, which is just not what it was supposed to be. It was supposed to be "something special," that thing you were looking forward to all through high school. Now you may see that it is nothing more than studying, tests, and confusion; pressures that can lead to self-medicating with food, sex, drugs, or alcohol; and a forced enthusiasm for "the home team," which may not be all that meaningful for you.

College, it turns out, is an inhibited life. There is a powerful felt unreality to what is indeed an unreal, artificial situation: sitting around for four years "studying." In those four years, you could establish a business, build a castle, discover a world, write a novel, connect the dots of the universe. Yet here you sit, studying for a test that could not feel more meaningless.

An example: for one undergraduate who is a chemistry major, these college years, even if in some ways meaningless, are at least made comprehensible by the fact that they are necessary steps in a career path. For another undergraduate, say a dance major, it is much less clear why she is there, given that she might be actually dancing in a real company rather than spending these prime years "preparing."

There are obvious "stressor" differences between the lives of, say, an undergraduate in physics, an undergraduate in software engineering, an undergraduate in political science who is already planning on heading to law school, and an undergraduate in English who is heading for poetry. The stress on the physics major may be primarily the hardness of the math she encounters, the stress on the engineering major may be primarily the sense that he could already be founding his start-up rather than wasting time in class, and so on. Each undergraduate finds herself squarely in her own particular bubble of stress.

There are also personality differences. The sort of person who gravitates toward one major is not the same sort of person who gravitates toward another major. A piano major is not the same sort of person as a business major, and a painting major is not the same sort of person as a biology pre-med major. They may all be smart, but they are not the same people. And still each one of them is likely to be encountering the same "dark night of the soul," that particular despair so common to the college years.

It goes without saying that a given smart teen may have an excellent college experience and that another smart teen may have at worst a neutral experience. But many smart teens will suffer, flounder, and crash. Between ten and fifteen percent of college freshmen report suicidal thinking, and suicide is the second leading cause of death among college students, after accidents. For each one of these ten or fifteen percent, how many more are despairing in their own way?

For Parents

You may hear from your smart teen who is away at college that "everything is fine." That is almost certainly not even close to the truth. She may be in the middle of coming out sexually and embroiled in her first tempestuous love affair, she may be frantically mulling over which major to choose, she may be hating her eating habits, her roommates, the dark winter, and her classes; she may be completely at sea. And still she is likely to say, "Everything is fine." Walk with her, be with her, spend some time being quiet with her, and see for yourself. She may be brewing enormous, life-changing decisions right at this moment. Be present for her, and give her the chance to begin a conversation.

For Teens

It is too small an answer to the problem I'm describing to say to you that you should watch your nutrition, make sure you get enough sleep, moderate your alcohol and drug consumption, use the counseling services that your college provides, and so on. These and the other excellent suggestions a counselor might make are not to be scorned. But they can't touch the beating heart of the problem.

At bottom is a challenge connected to the very fabric of what it is like for you to be nineteen, smart, confused, dark, roiling, and trapped in a dorm room with others just as troubled as you. I beg you to commit to meeting that challenge by surviving your college years. Here is the big news: there is a good life coming, one that will feel completely different from the one you are currently experiencing.

IN CONCLUSION

If you're the parent of a smart teen, I hope that this book has helped you gain a better understanding of how your smart teen is experiencing life, what special challenges she faces, and how you might help her meet these real, pressing challenges. They can only be met imperfectly, but it is infinitely better to meet a challenge imperfectly than to leave it unaddressed. One conversation can make a huge difference. I hope that I've pointed you to the kinds of conversation that you and your teen might have.

If you're a smart teen, I hope that I've spoken to you. We have countless ways of naming, labeling, thinking about, and describing what ails human beings. These many ways tend to objectify the individual, picturing him as "someone with depression," "an addict," "having a behavior problem," "having a borderline personality," and so on. But that isn't how life looks or feels to you, is it?

You are inside the race car, rushing around the track, not in the announcer's booth, reporting on the race. You feel the track's turns, you feel the power of the engine, you hear the grinding of gears, you feel the presence and the pressure of the other cars around you. The announcer may blandly report that you are five seconds behind the leader—but inside, what a wild ride you're experiencing!

You know that worry about a test can make you sick. You know how hard it is to walk down the school corridors after you've embarrassed yourself. You know the fierce pull in you to be reckless. You know what it feels like to be surrounded by hypocrisy and to want to scream. You know how easy it is to go down one rabbit hole after another, spending hours lost who knows where. You know what it feels like to not have a date, to feel unwanted, to not even feel much like living. You know these things.

That was my first goal in writing this book, to be "inside" with you, inside where you actually are, not writing to you but experiencing life with you. I hope you've felt that. My second goal was to help you think about the ways that being smart plays itself out, how native intelligence creates predictable challenges. We've looked at your particular hungers, at your stubborn individuality, at that special god-bug anxiety that wells up in you because you feel both special and damaged. We looked at many things—forty-eight sections' worth. You might want to revisit the sections that spoke to you the most—there may be more for you to learn there and experience there.

I hope that this book has helped you identify your challenges and provided you with some part-answers and food for thought. We both know that there is a build-up inside of you that may express itself in ways called "depression" and "anxiety" and "hyperactivity" and "addiction." I hope that I've given you more than labels to attach to your thoughts, feelings, and behaviors. I hope that I've provided you with a picture of a life—your life.

You are not on a pedestal, and you are not at the pinnacle of the species. You are just a person. But your smarts can help us all. There is no universal arbiter of meaning or purpose, and so you will have to decide for yourself if you care to be of help. If you do care to be of assistance to humanity, we need you at your best. We need you to weather the challenges that everyone must face and to weather your own special challenges as well. I hope that this book helps you do just that.

Some of my other books may also speak to you, and reading one or another of them might constitute your next step. Whether you're a smart teen, the parent of a smart teen, an educator, a coach, a therapist, or simply someone interested in this fascinating species of ours, I hope that you've found this book interesting and useful. You can be in touch with me; send any thoughts, comments, or questions to me at ericmaisel@hotmail.com. Please do be in touch. I'd especially love to hear your story. And you might be interested in the prequel to this book, *Why Smart People Hurt*. That book might also serve you.

ABOUT THE AUTHOR

Eric Maisel, PhD, is the author of more than fifty books in the areas of creativity, psychology, coaching, mental health, and cultural trends. He is a psychotherapist and the founder of the creativity coach profession, regularly working with lawyers, doctors, scientists, writers, painters, business people, and folks from every walk of life. They include folks settled in a profession as well as folks struggling to find an outlet for their intelligence and looking for work that will allow them to be as smart as they are. They include individuals who are successful in their careers and those who, because of the realities of the marketplace, struggle to achieve success. And through his books, they could include you.

Sought after as an expert in his field, Dr. Maisel regularly contributes to Mad in America, writes a monthly print column for *Professional Artist* magazine, and writes the *Rethinking Mental Health* blog for Psychology Today. He has been the keynote speaker at many conferences and leads Deep Writing workshops worldwide.

Dr. Maisel currently resides in Walnut Creek, California. Visit him at www.ericmaisel.com.

Mango Publishing, established in 2014, publishes an eclectic list of books by diverse authors—both new and established voices—on topics ranging from business, personal growth, women's empowerment, LGBTQ studies, health, and spirituality to history, popular culture, time management, decluttering, lifestyle, mental wellness, aging, and sustainable living. We were recently named 2019 *and* 2020's #1 fastest-growing independent publisher by *Publishers Weekly*. Our success is driven by our main goal, which is to publish high-quality books that will entertain readers as well as make a positive difference in their lives.

Our readers are our most important resource; we value your input, suggestions, and ideas. We'd love to hear from you— after all, we are publishing books for you!

Please stay in touch with us and follow us at:
    Facebook: Mango Publishing
    Twitter: @MangoPublishing
    Instagram: @MangoPublishing
    LinkedIn: Mango Publishing
    Pinterest: Mango Publishing
    Newsletter: mangopublishinggroup.com/newsletter

Join us on Mango's journey to reinvent publishing, one book at a time.

CPSIA information can be obtained
at www.ICGtesting.com
Printed in the USA
JSHW042245010722
27741JS00002B/2